VB Scripting for CATIA V5

How to Program CATIA Macros

Emmett Ross

Third Edition

Table of Contents

Copyright Information

Disclaimer

Although the author has attempted to exhaustively research all sources to ensure the accuracy and completeness of information on the subject matter, the author assumes no responsibility for errors, inaccuracies, omissions, or any other inconsistencies herein. The data contained herein is for informational purposes only and is not represented to be error free. Information may be rendered inaccurate by changes made to the subject of the material, such as the applicable software. No consequential damages can be sought against the author for the use of these materials by any third parties or for any direct or indirect result of that use. The purpose of this text is to complement and supplement other texts and resources. You are urged to read all the available literature, learn as much as you can and adapt the information to your particular needs. There may be mistakes within this manual. Therefore, the text should only be used as a general and introductory guide and not as the sole source for CATIA macro programming. The information contained herein is intended to be of general interest to you and is provided "as is", and it does not address the circumstances of any particular individual or entity. Nothing herein constitutes professional advice, nor does it constitute a comprehensive or complete statement of the issues discussed thereto.

The author also assumes a general understanding of how to use CATIA V5 including geometry creation and various workbenches (mainly Part Design, Generative Shape Design, and Assembly Design). To learn more about CATIA please refer to the resources in the Appendix for more information about how to use CATIA or where to go to get further answers or advice. I welcome any comments you may have regarding this book. To contact me please email: emmett@scripting4v5.com

The Author's Story

Learning how to program CATIA macros helped save my career.

You've probably found your way to this book from my website, or maybe a friend passed it along to you. Either way, I'm happy you're here. I wrote this guide because when I was in a time of desperate need, not too long ago, learning how to write CATIA macros helped save my professional career. I was working as a CAD engineer but was just beginning to learn how to use CATIA. Everyone else at my company was much more experienced than I was, therefore I was expendable. When the economy took a turn for the worse, and coworkers began getting laid off, I feared for my job and my family's future.

I needed a way to set myself apart to prove my value to the team. Learning how to write macros in CATIA gave me a huge advantage over my coworkers and helped to quickly earn my colleague's respect, leading not only to me keeping the job but also to quicker promotions, along with more job freedom and flexibility. Not only did it help me bounce back from a low point but it opened my eyes to the world of automation and the opportunities that it can create for an engineer's career. *Scripting4v5.com* and *VB Scripting for CATIA V5* are my way of giving back for all of the fortunate things that have happened to me ever since.

This eBook is a guide, and the purpose of this guide is to do just that - ***guide you***. It will, however, take you through the process of taking the ideas and knowledge in your head, putting them together and sharing that with the world. If I can help just one person learn one thing that will help them in their career and/or life, the past several months I have spent writing this eBook will have been totally worth it. If at any point while you're reading this guide and you have any questions, please don't hesitate to contact me. Even if you don't have any questions, I'd love for you to come by and say hello! If you want to reach me in private you can email me at emmett@scripting4v5.com.

-Emmett Ross

Chapter 1: Introduction to CATIA Programming

Are you tired of repeating those same time-consuming CATIA processes over and over? Worn out by thousands of mouse clicks? Don't you wish there were a better way to do things? What if you could rid yourself those hundreds of headaches by teaching yourself how to program macros while impressing your bosses and coworkers in the process? **VB Scripting for CATIA V5** is the internet's most complete guide to teach you how to write macros for CATIA V5!

Through a series of example codes and tutorials you'll learn how to unleash the full power and potential of CATIA V5. No programming experience is required! There are many CAD engineers, designers, and technicians who want to write macros but simply don't have the time or money to go to an expensive third party training class. This text will cover the core items to help teach beginners important concepts needed to create custom CATIA macros. More importantly, you'll learn how to solve problems and what to do when you get stuck. Once you begin to see the patterns you'll be flying along on your own in no time.

This book contains step-by-step tutorials labeled as Workshops. There are also exercises where you are given an end goal and a brief outline of a problem that you must then come up with the code solution on your own. The solutions for each exercise are located in the back of the book.

What is a Macro and why do we use them?

A macro is a series of functions written in a scripting language that is grouped in a single command to perform the requested task automatically. If you perform a task repeatedly you can take advantage of a macro to automate the task. Macros are used to save time and reduce the possibility of human error by automating repetitive processes, standardization, improving efficiency, expanding CATIA's capabilities, and by streamlining procedures. Macros use programming but you don't need to be a programmer or have programming knowledge to use them (though it does help).

The application of automation in the design process is virtually unlimited. Some real world examples of CATIA automation at work:

- Batch script for the conversion of CATDrawing files to PDF
- Import of points from an Excel spreadsheet to a 3D CAD model
- Export of data from CATIA model to a bill of material spreadsheet
- Automatic geometry creation from selection
- Automatic drawing creation

And so on and so on. The possibilities are nearly limitless.

Terms and Definitions

The following is a list of terms and their definitions which will be used frequently throughout this text. It is recommended that you become familiar with them if you aren't already. A quick reference of acronyms is listed in the appendices of this book as well.

Integrated Development Environment (IDE) is a computer application to help programmers develop software and typically consists of a source code editor, debugger, build automation tools, object browser, and a compiler or interpreter. Typically have built-in syntax checkers, color coded schemes, and code completion.

Graphical User Interface (GUI) is a way for humans to interact with computers with graphical elements such as windows, menus, toolbars, icons, etc. which can be manipulated by a mouse. The VBA editor is a perfect example.

Command Line Interface (CLI) is a way for humans to interact with computers through text only and is accessed solely by a keyboard. The most common example is MS-DOS.

Component Application Architecture (CAA, CAA V5, or CNext) is the **Application Programming Interface (API)** or technological infrastructure designed to support Dassault Systèmes products. It is an open development platform enabling programmers to develop and integrate their own applications for CATIA or other Dassault Systèmes products. CAA V5 is faster and more powerful than VB. It provides access to interfaces not available to Visual Basic but harder to learn. C++ is the primary language. A single source code is used for both Windows and UNIX. CAA **Rapid Application Development Environment (RADE)** provides a workbench to develop PLM applications using the component object model object oriented programming. CAA is beyond the scope of this text.

Object Oriented Programming (OOP) is where programmers define not only the data type of a data structure, but also the types of operations, or functions, that can be applied to the data structure. An object in software is a structure that consists of data fields and subroutines or functions. Everything in CATIA is an object; the data fields are called *Properties* and the subroutines and functions are called *Methods*. All the data and functions have owners which are the objects to which they belong. A thorough understanding of OOP is critical to your success in macro programming.

Component Object Model (COM) is a Microsoft technology that enables sharing of binary code across different applications and languages. CATIA V5 is COM enabled software. Codes for COM objects or components can be called, initiated, or created at any time because they are stored in DLL files and registered in the Windows registry. If CATIA calls Excel, CATIA is then the client and Excel is the server, or the one that provides *services* to the client.

VB talks to CATIA through **Dynamic Linked Libraries (DLL).** DLLs are compiled files that contain all of the functions that make CATIA V5 perform an action. For example, when you select the "point" function in CATIA, the program calls a function inside one of the dll files that performs the action of creating a point in the V5 database. These files are both compiled and encrypted (or "mangled") and are located in the UNLOAD directory for CATIA V5 (*C:\Program Files\Dassault Systemes\B20\intel_1\code\bin*). Encryption is a method by which software companies can ensure that others cannot access the function inside the dlls. You cannot directly call the dlls from outside applications, therefore extra programming needs to be done to allow the dlls to be exposed to Windows and the COM object model. This is done via Type Library Files.

Type Library Files (TLB) are files necessary for exposing functions to Windows by acting as maps which point to the functions inside of the dll files that make CATIA V5 work. The TLB files are also located in the UNLOAD directory for V5. Any external application needs to have access to these files. The complete process is: VB Application -> Type Libraries -> Dynamic Linked Libraries -> CNext. How to create references to type libraries is shown in later chapters of this text.

Universal Unique Identifier (UUID) - Every CATPart and CATProduct contains a UUID. Basically, CATIA identifies files based on their file name and their UUID. Where problems occur are when two pieces of data have the same UUID. Compounding the problem, the UUID can't be viewed or edited with any current CATIA function. There are cases when two files may have different names but share the same UUID. This causes a problem when dealing with **Product Data Management (PDM)** systems, like SmartTeam. It is recommended to create new UUIDs whenever possible. Actions which will **create new UUID** include:

- File + New
- File + New From
- File + SaveAs - option save as new document
- INSERT New Product
- INSERT New Part
- Document Template Creation

Actions which will **keep the same UUID** for each include:

- File + Open
- File + Save Management
- File + Save
- File + SaveAs
- Send to directory
- File + CLOSE
- File + Save
- File + Save ALL

CATIA Macro Languages

CATIA V5 automation was originally designed for VB6, VBA, and VBScript. Microsoft no longer officially supports VB6 as it has been replaced by VB.net, which is supported by CATIA V5 R16 and onwards. VB6 is more complex but more powerful than VBA, as is VBA over VBScript and CATScript. Macro languages supported by CATIA and discussed in this text are VBScript, CATScript, and VBA, all derivatives of Visual Basic used in scripting.

CATScript is Dassault Systèmes' portable version of VBScript and is very similar to it. CATScript macros CAN run on UNIX systems. It is a sequential programming language and non-GUI oriented. Regular text editors (like Notepad) can be used for coding. Advantages of writing CATScript macros include free to use, macro recording, personal time saving operations, and rapid deployment. The disadvantages of CATScript are limited flexibility and difficult to debug. The file extension is **.CATScript**.

VBScript is a subset of the Visual Basic Programming language (VBA). All elements of VBScript are present in VBA, but some VBA elements are not implemented in VBScript. The result of the slimming down process is a very small language that is easy to use. VBScript (officially, "Microsoft Visual Basic Scripting Edition") was originally designed to run in Web applications such as Internet Explorer. One of the advantages of VBScript (in common with other scripting languages) is that it's written in plain, ordinary ASCII text. That means that your 'development environment' can be something as simple as Notepad. CATIA objects can be called but no type is used as the system tries to dynamically call methods and properties of objects. It can be used on both Windows and UNIX versions of CATIA. The disadvantage of VBScript is it's slow, is limited for interface development, and has the least functionality. The file extension is **.catvbs**.

VBScript (MS VBScript) and CATScript are very similar with the major difference being variable declaration. I personally believe it is better to declare all variables As String, As Integer, etc.) to better keep track of each variable type.

Visual Basic (VB or VB6) is the full and complete version. Derived from BASIC, VB6 programs can generate independent programs, can create ActiveX and servers, and can be compiled. VB programs run in their own memory space.

VBA (Visual Basic for Applications) is another subset of Visual Basic and is hosted in applications such as CATIA (after V5R8), Microsoft Word, Excel, etc. VBA provides a complete programming environment with an editor, debugger, and help object viewer. Declaring the object library used is allowed. In CATIA, VBA has the full VB6 syntax and IDE, which is similar to VBA in Excel. It is event driven; GUI oriented, and has full IDE yet cannot run a program WITHOUT the host application running (meaning it runs as a DLL in the same memory space as the host application). The advantages of using CATvba macros include using the GUI, building forms, and the debugging ability of the macro editor. The disadvantage is VBA programs cannot be compiled into executables or DLLs and they do not run in their own memory space. The extension is **.catvba**.

Visual Basic.NET (VB.net) is Microsoft's designated successor to VB6 and has been supported by Dassault Systèmes since V5R16. VB.net is event driven, has IDE, and is used for building GUI but is not COM (though it can call COM objects). The syntax is different from VB6. Code can be compiled into .exe or .asp files. There are many issues encountered when switching from VB6 to VB.net, such as new syntax, new IDE, new GUI controls, and a new Install Shield, therefore fully automatic conversions are near impossible. Compiled languages like VB.net aren't completely necessary because most automation can be done in VBA. VB.net will not be discussed in this text.

There are two primary methods a macro communicates with CATIA: in-process or out of process.

In Process: The first method a macro communicates with CATIA is when the VB application is ran from within the CATIA process in the computer memory. CATIA essentially freezes while the macro is running and the allocation memory is wiped clean after each run of the program so passing data between subsequent runs is impossible. To access and create in-process macros go to Tools > Macros but please note the only options are VBScript, CATScript, or VBA.

Out of Process: The other communication method is called out of process where the program runs in its own process in the computer memory. The application could be run from Excel, Word, Windows Explorer, etc. CATIA is fully active while the program is running. VB.net or VB6 can also be used.

How to Create Macros

Macros within CATIA are created by two primary methods:

1. Using the macro recorder or
2. Writing custom code with the macro editor

Once a macro is created, there are multiple ways to open the macros window to run your macros:

1. Go to Tools>Macro>Macros
2. Use the Macros toolbar
3. Keyboard shortcut: **Alt+F8**
4. Create your own icon for each macro

If the macro editor cannot be opened you should talk to your system administrator because it may not have been installed. No extra license is required to run macros, though sometimes licenses for special workbenches are needed if the code uses a function or method from a particular workbench.

Macro Libraries

CATIA macros are stored in macro libraries in one of three locations: Folders (vbscript and CATScript), Project files (catvba), or CATParts/CATProducts. Only one of these macro libraries can be used at a time. When creating a new macro library, the folder or path location must already exist. If not you will get an error message. Use the following steps to create a new macro library or setup an existing one:

1. Go to Tools>Macro>Macros
2. Click "Macro libraries..."
3. Make sure the Library type is set to "Directories" then click "Add existing library..."
4. Browse to "C:\MyCatScripts" or wherever your CATScripts are saved then click ok or create a new library.
5. Close the macros libraries window. If setting up an existing library you should see a list of .CATScript files. You only need to do this once as the library should load even after restarting CATIA.

Macro Recording

One method for creating macros is by recording your mouse actions. For macros recorded in a folder or in a CATPart or CATProduct, Dim statements (declarations) will be recorded for CATScript but not for MSVBScript. For macros recorded in a .catvba library, "MS VBA" is the only choice. Macros **cannot** be recorded while in the drafting workbench. A few things to keep in mind when recording a macro:

DON'T: Switch workbenches while recording a macro.
DON'T: Record more than is absolutely necessary.
DON'T: Use the UNDO button when recording a macro.
DO: Be aware of CATSettings when recording.
DO: Exit sketches before stopping recording.
DO: Check each macro after it's recorded.

Always UNDO what you just recorded and run the macro (you are able to undo CATIA macros after you've run them which is a good way to check if they work as expected or not). If the macro works from within CATIA and repeats what you just did, then the macro obviously works fine. If it does NOT work from within CATIA, you need to fix it. If it does NOT work from within CATIA it will NOT work once you cut and paste it into a VB application.

Look through the recorded macro. Many times extra lines of code are added which are not necessary. This is based on the order of steps that you do as you record the macro. These unnecessary lines can be removed. Recorded macros do not contain any comments or explanations of what is happening in the code and input parameters are never recorded.

For example, a macro is recorded to zoom in and then zoom out it might display the following code:

```
Dim viewpoint3D As Viewpoint3D
Set viewpoint3D = viewer3D.Viewpoint3D
Viewer3D.ZoomIn
Set viewpoint3D = viewer3D.Viewpoint3D
Viewer3D.ZoomOut
Set viewpoint3D = viewer3D.Viewpoint3D
```

Notice how the "Set Viewpoint" command appears multiple times? This is unnecessary in this situation. The viewpoint only needs to be set once after the Dim statement (setting and declaring will be explained in more detail in the upcoming chapters).

Often times you might record a macro with a CATPart active and open it in its own window. All goes smoothly and the macro replays fine. Then, the next day you replay the macro again but this time you may have some other document type open or maybe a part is open but it is in a product assembly. Usually, the macro will fail because when the code was recorded a CATPart was the active document but now it is not. You need to add your own error handling to the code to ensure this doesn't happen. This is one advantage to writing custom code and knowing the fundamentals of CATIA macro programming.

Create a Macro Icon

To create an icon for each macro go to Tools>Customize>Commands tab> scroll down to Macros>click "Show Properties." Under Commands, select the macro then click the "…" box. The icon browser pops up. There are over 6,000 unique icons to choose from. Select one then hit Close. Finally, drag and drop the macro file from the command window to whatever toolbar you would like the icon to appear on (such as "Graphic Properties" or create a new one). Now you can click the Icon to run your macro! You can also setup custom keyboard shortcuts from within the same window as well.

Workshop 1: Fundamentals

Follow the step-by-step instructions of Workshop 1.

WORKSHOP 1

Fundamentals

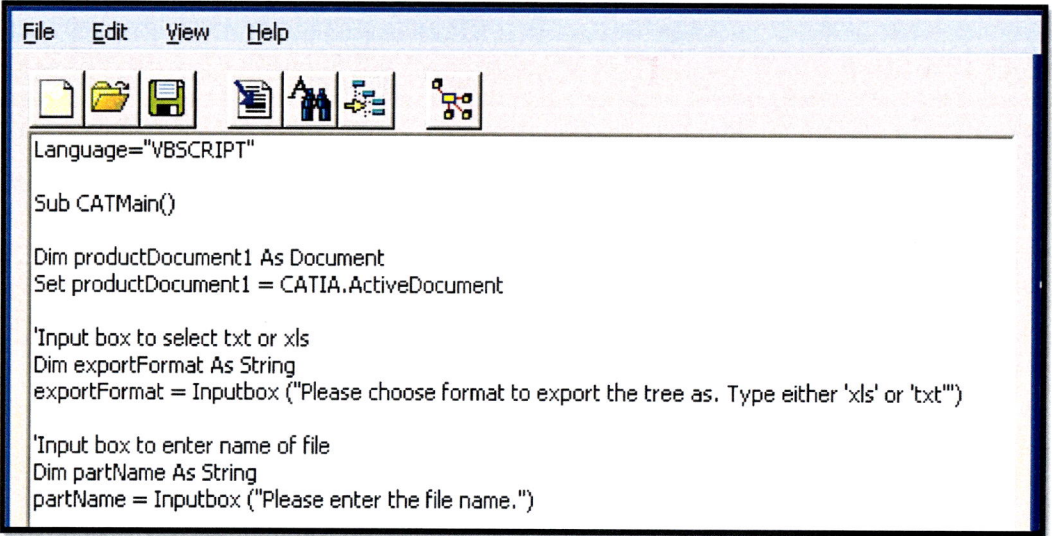

Workshop 1 – Introduction

- ## Description

VBScript is a subset of the Visual Basic Programming language (VBA). All elements of VBScript are present in VBA, but some VBA elements are not implemented in VBScript. The result of the slimming down process is a very small language that is easy to use. In this workshop you will learn some of the basic fundamentals needed to create and run macros.

- ## Outline

1. How to add a macro library
2. How to open and run macros
3. How to create an icon for your macros
4. Create a "hello" message box macro

Why use macros?

Save time and reduce the possibility of human error by automating repetitive processes.

- Standardization
- Improve efficiency
- Expand CATIA capabilities
- Streamline tasks

Macros in CATIA are created by two primary methods:

1. Macro recorder
2. Write custom code with the macro editor

How to add a macro library

Use the following steps to setup an existing macro library:

Go to Tools>Macro>Macros

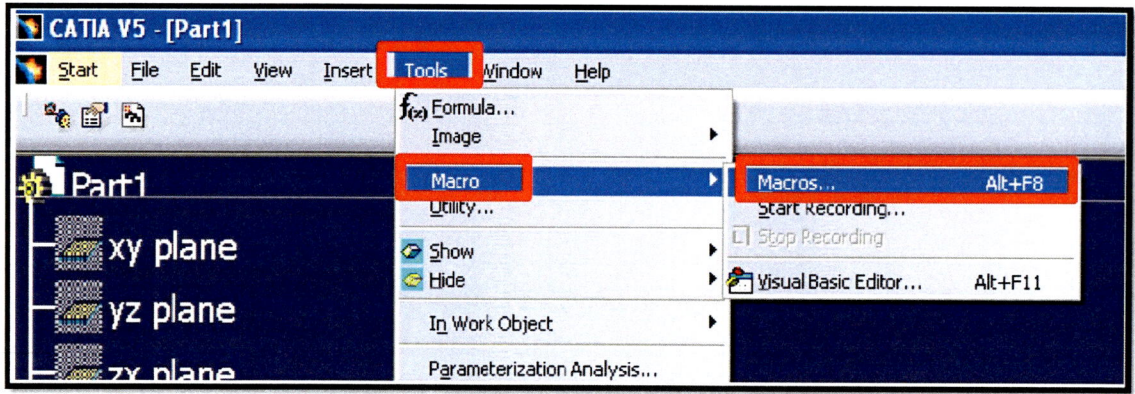

•Click "Macro libraries..."

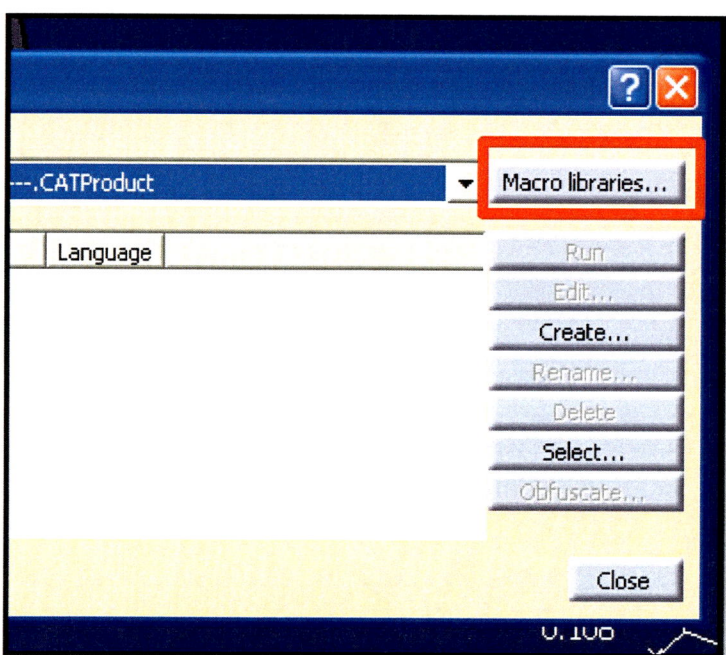

Make sure the Library type is set to "Directories" then click "Add existing library..."

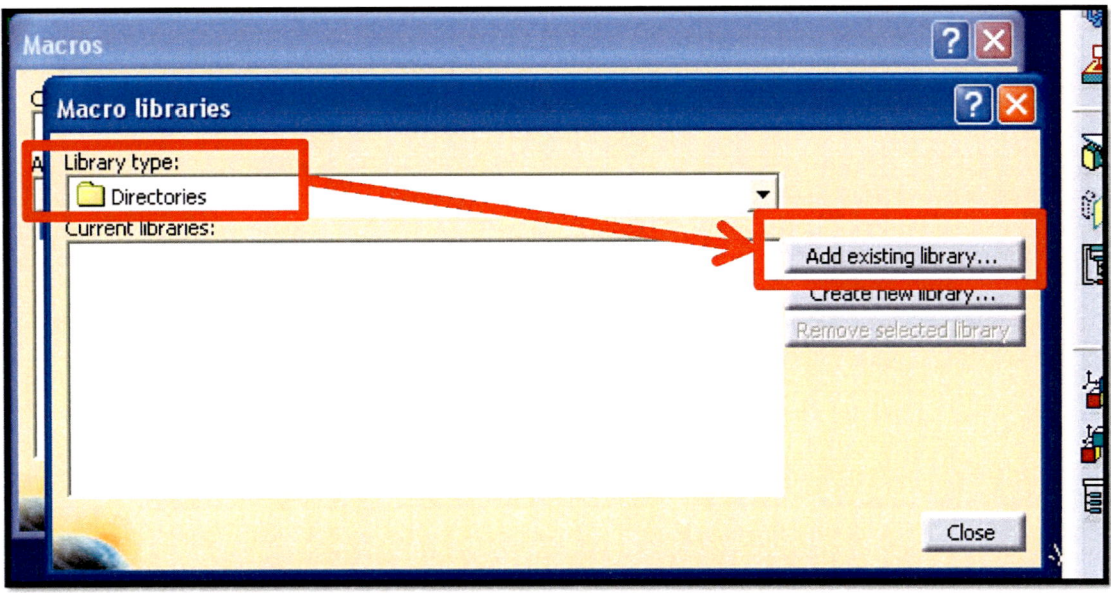

Browse to "C:\MyCatScripts" or wherever your macros are saved then click ok.

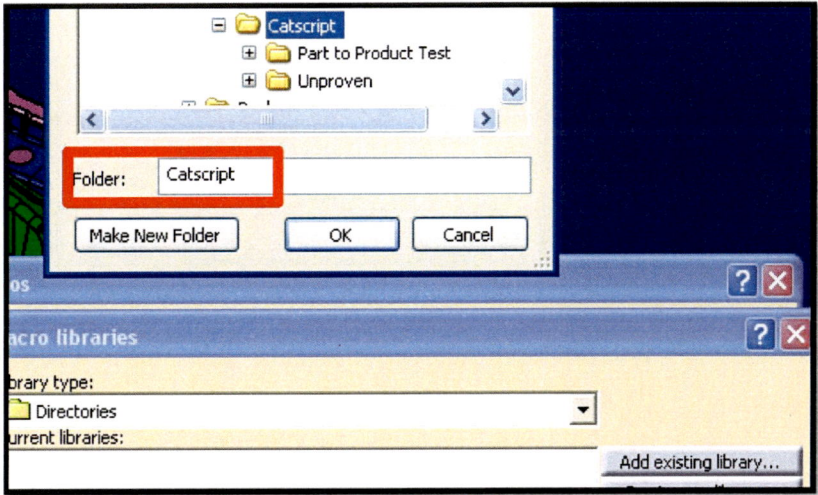

Close the macros libraries window.

After you have created some macros you will see a list of the .CATscript files here.

You only need to do this once- the library should load even after restarting CATIA.

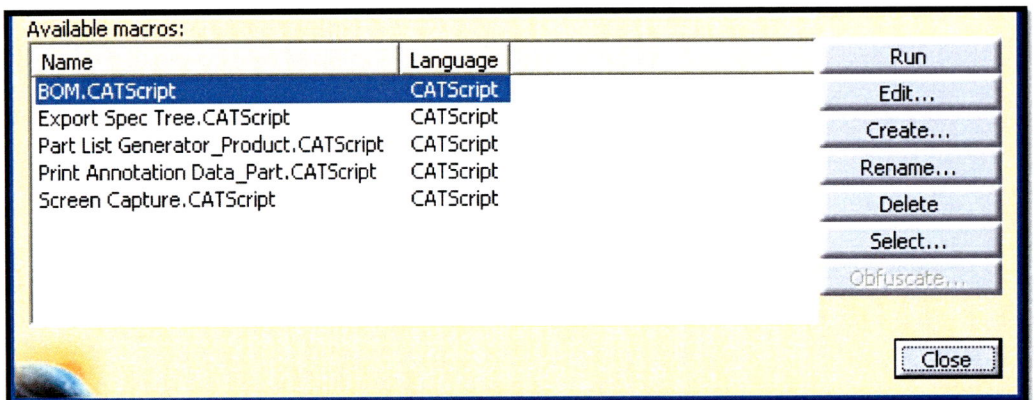

To open and run macros

There are multiple ways to open the macros window:

- Tools>Macro>Macros
- Macros toolbar
- Keyboard shortcut: **Alt+F8**
- Create your own icon for each macro

Recording a Macro

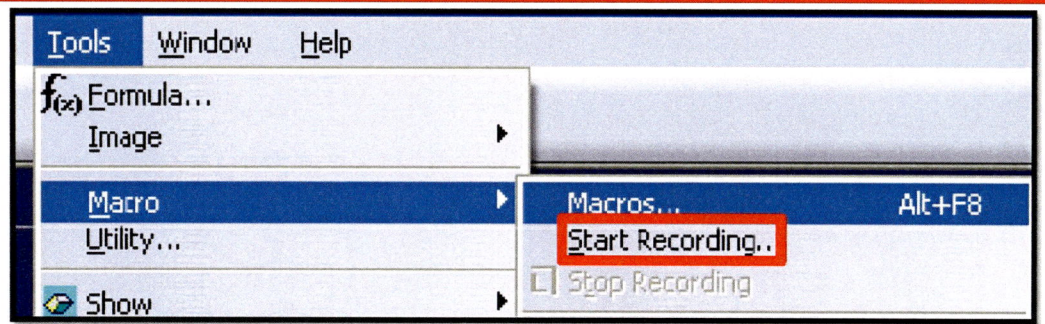

To record a macro go to:
Tools>Macro>Start Recording…
Pick a library, language, and macro name.

To stop recording:
Tools>Macro>Stop Recording or click the stop button

To create an icon for each macro:

Go to Tools>Customize>Commands tab> scroll down to
Macros>click "Show Properties"

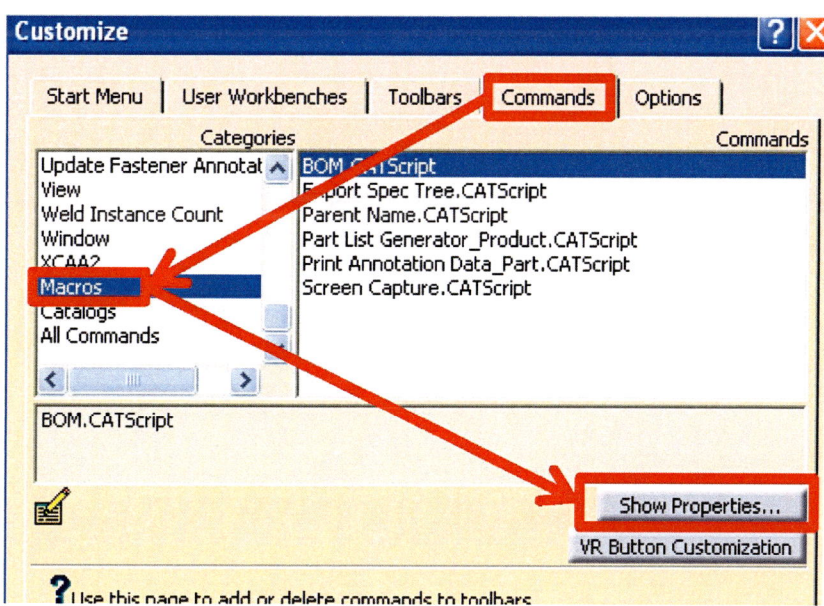

Under Commands, select the macro then click the "..." box. The icon browser pops up. Over 6000 to choose from. Select one then hit close.

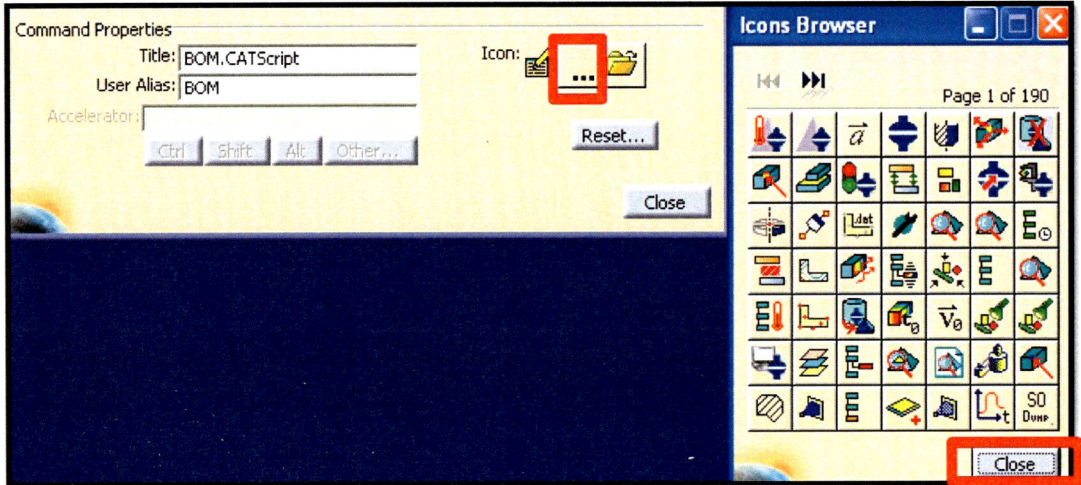

- Finally, drag and drop the .CATScript file from the command window to whatever toolbar you would like the icon to appear on
- Now you can click the Icon to run your macro!
- You can also setup a custom keyboard shortcut as well.
- Code can be sent to other user as a lightweight .txt text file

Fundamentals Example

Hit **alt+F8** to open the macro window. Create a new CATScript macro named msgbox. Click the Edit button. Type the code below. The following code will display a message box with the text "Hello." strHello is a variable declared as a string (or text) object. strHello is then defined. Every Sub must end with "End Sub". Click Save. Close the editor and run your macro. The "Hello" message box should appear.

```
Sub CATMain()
    Dim strHello As String
    strHello="Hello"
    MsgBox strHello
End Sub
```

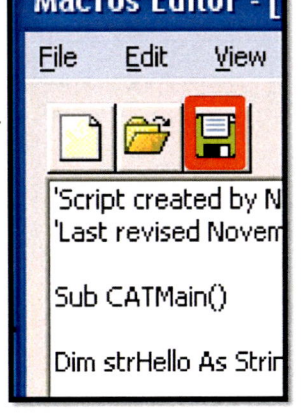

Workshop 1 – Conclusion

This concludes workshop 1. In this workshop you have learned to:

•Create a new macro
•Create an icon for your macro
•How to record a macro
•Create a "Hello" message box

CATIA Macro Syntax

Syntax is defined as the ordering of and relationship between the words and other structural elements in phrases and sentences. You can think of it as a particular layout of words and symbols. Each scripting language is composed of its own syntax. Learning the syntax of each programming language is crucial to creating successful macros. Think of it like this: when you see an email address (emmett@scripting4v5.com) you immediately identify it as an email address. Why is this? An email address has a correct structure in the language of the internet, its syntax. Syntax enables the programming language to understand what it is you are trying to do. Listed below are some of the key syntax features of CATIA macro programming:

- **Case Sensitivity:** By default, VBA is not case sensitive and does not differentiate between upper-case and lower-case spelling of words.
- **Comments:** Add comments to your statements using an apostrophe ('), either at the beginning of a separate line, or at the end of a statement. It is recommended that you add comments wherever possible to make your scripts easier to understand and maintain, especially if another user has to make changes to it later on down the road.
- **Indentation:** Indent or out dent script to reflect the logical structure and nesting of the statements to make it easier to read.
- **Parentheses:** To achieve the desired result and to avoid errors, it is important to use parentheses correctly in any statement.
- **Semicolon (:):** Inserting a semicolon allows you to write multiple commands on the same line of code.
- **Single Quotation('):** To return a single quotation mark which does not indicate a comment needed in a formula for example, you'll have to use the Chr function. Chr() is a built-in VBA function that returns the character that corresponds to the numeric value of its argument, using the ASCII coding scheme. If you provide Chr with an integer value (such as 39) it will report back the character that corresponds to that value. The ASCII value of 39 is the single quote mark. Chr(34) is for the double quote mark. This is shown in an example later on in this text.
- **Spaces:** Add extra blank spaces to your script to improve clarity. These spaces are ignored by VBA.
- **Text Strings:** When a value is entered as a text string you must add quotation marks before and after the string. You can concatenate, or combine, multiple strings using a plus (+) or ampersand (&) sign: txtString = "This value is "+ TestValue. Return the left, middle, or right of a string using: left(sting, digits), mid(string, digits), or right(string, digits). Get the complete length of a string with len(string). To figure out if a string contains another string use Instr(). Convert numeric strings and vice versa using str(num) or val(string).
- **Underscore(_):** Carry over to next line (line concatenation symbol)

Syntax is often the biggest cause of a macro program giving an error and not working. There is a correct way to write your code. It takes practice, patience, and persistence to understand but over time it will become second nature to you. If you follow the rules the programming languages will understand you otherwise you will get errors.

Dealing with syntax can be tough which is why programmers have developed tools to help create programs correctly. These are called IDE, or integrated development environments (remember that definition I defined earlier?). The Visual Basic editor in CATIA is the perfect example (Alt+F11). It contains a built-in syntax checker and works much like a grammar checker found in software like Microsoft Word and will even give you hints about what it *thinks* you meant.

CATIA Macro Variable Naming

Variables make up the backbone of any programming language. Basically, variables store information that can be accessed later by referring to a name or "variable." Let's say you have an input box in your code where the user will enter a part number. You refer to the input box as componentName. In other words, componentName is a symbolic name, or word, for the input box, the variable. You can then ask the question in your code "What value does the variable componentName contain?" Variables can then be declared as a type to let us know what we can do with that information (discussed in more detail in the next chapter). The value of a variable will not necessarily be constant throughout the duration a program is running.

How you decide to name your variables is very important. In the previous example, instead of giving the input box a variable name of "componentName" we could have called it "ImASuperAwesomeProgrammer." However, this doesn't make a lot of sense and doesn't help us, especially if we're looking at the code months from now or another programmer has to modify the code.

There are a few rules we must follow. Variable names, also known as identifiers, must be less than 255 characters, they cannot start with a number, and special characters, such as spaces and periods, are forbidden. Avoid naming conflicts. Two variables cannot have the same name.

Good Variable Names: dimensionOne, dimension1

Bad Variable Names: dimension One, 1dimension

There is a naming convention called "Hungarian notation" where a letter is placed in front of the variable name to notate what type of data the variable is. For example:

- o= object (i.e. oPartDoc)
- str=string (i.e. strFilename)
- i=integer (i.e iCount)
- rng=Range (i.e. rngField)

Many programmers use "int" or "n" for integer and "s" for string. Either or works as long as your notation is consistent and easy for others to understand then it doesn't matter what notation you use.

Program Structure and Format

Macros in CATIA use **sequential programming**, meaning when you run your macro program, the code will be read by the computer line by line, generally from top to bottom and from left to right, just like reading a book. The program flows down the code until it hits a decision point where it may have to jump to different portion of the program or re-run lines of code that it already read. The program chooses what lines of code to execute based on the state of the variables you have defined.

Macros can also be **event driven** meaning the execution of the program depends on an event, such as a user clicking a button with the mouse, an object being selected, certain text or characters being typed into a form, etc. One common decision point is an If...Else statement. If the variable equals x then do y, else do z. Another one is the while loop which will execute the lines of code within the loop over and over until the condition becomes false. There are more examples of decision points and control structures but we'll get to those later on in the text.

I strive to remain consistent on my CATIA macro format and you should too. Try to keep the same format and order on every single program you create. It's very useful to keep your code clean and tidy, especially if other programmers are going to work on it later. Remember; keep the code as simple as possible. Always try to use as few lines of code as possible (which you'll be glad you did when you have to troubleshoot one of your macros). You can reduce the number of lines of code using a colon (:). The macro format I use looks something like this:

```
'my name
'date last revised
'who the macro was created for
'description of what the macro does
'————-separator————-
Main code begins here, usually with Sub CATMain
        'define variables, constants, etc.
        'error handling
        'check if part or product is in design mode or not
        'update part, drawing, etc.
        'double check to make sure all loops are closed
End Sub
```

Create Your First Macro

It's time to follow along to create our first CATIA macro. Create a new library and a new macro.

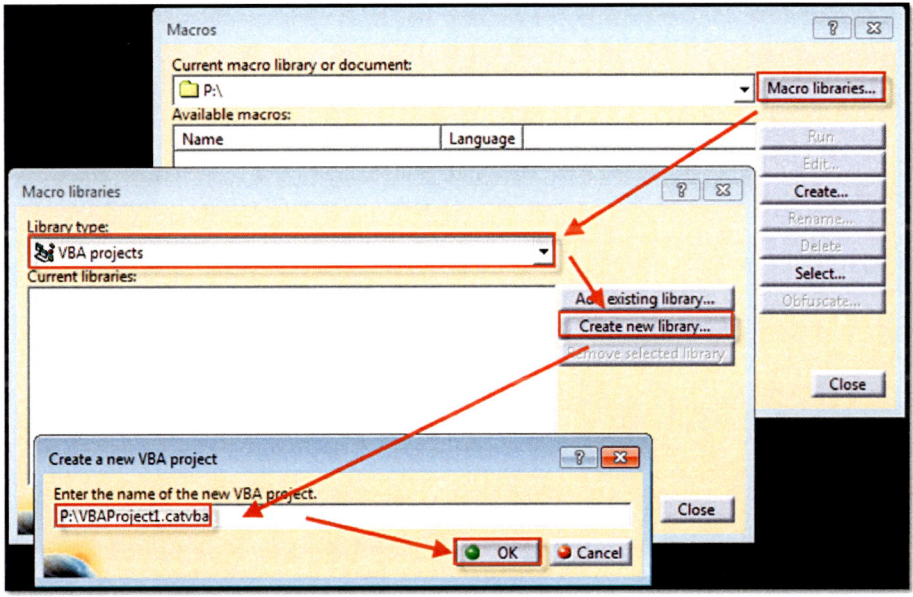

Create a new macro using the MS VBA language (most examples in this book are either VBA or CATScript).

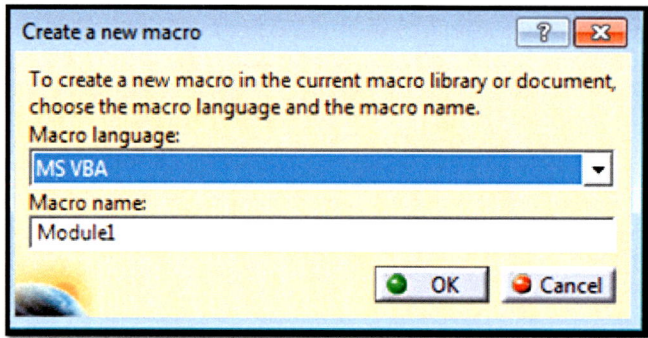

Rename the macro to Exercise1 then double click or hit edit to begin editing the macro in the VBA editor.

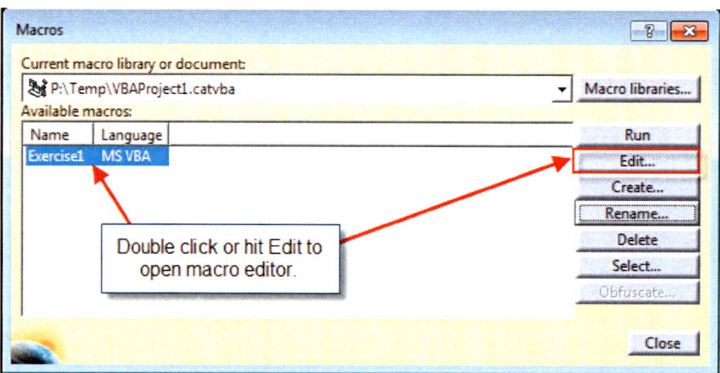

Go to Tools > References and make sure all available CATIA references are selected.

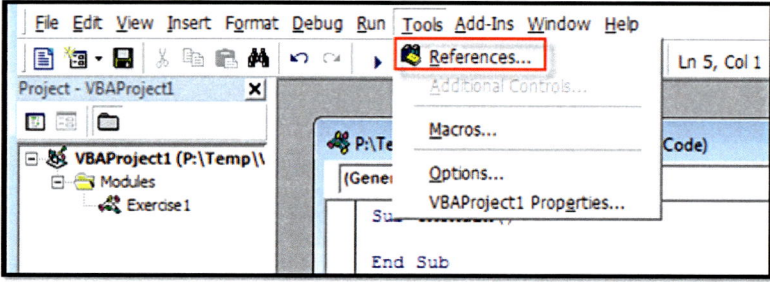

By default, CATIA doesn't force you to declare your variables. However, you should change that setting immediately. In CATIA (or Excel or other software), press Alt+F11 to launch the Visual Basic Editor (VBE). Go to Tools>Options.

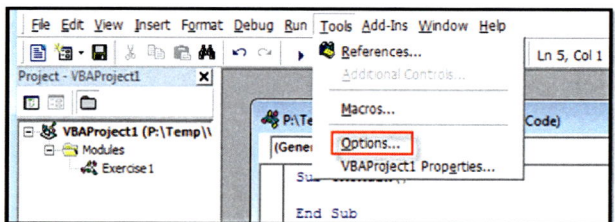

In the Editor tab of the Options dialog, make sure that there's a check mark in front of *"Require Variable Declaration"*

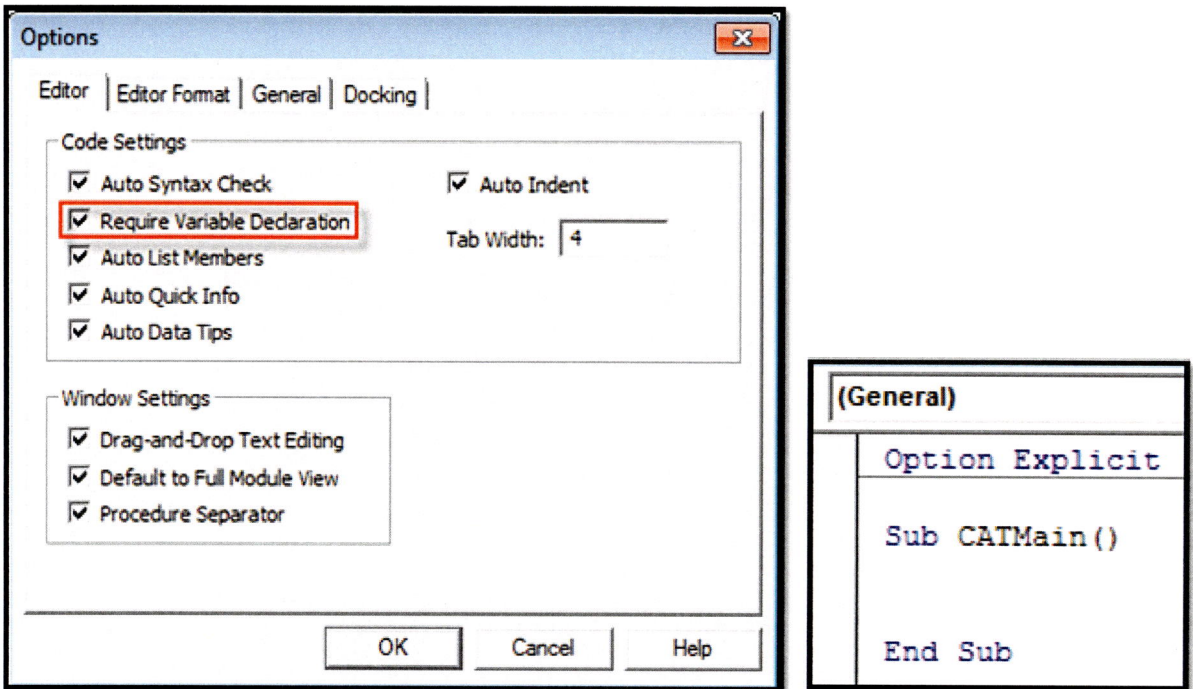

After you click OK, insert a new Module. When you do so, you'll see Option Explicit as the first line of the module. This line tells CATIA that all variables must be declared making your code easier to read and follow. Option Explicit will be the first line in our code.

A CATIA VB program or "macro" consists of a "Subroutine" named CATMain(). CATIA only recognizes Sub CATMain as the entry point to any VBA application. Every Sub must end with an End Sub.

```
Option Explicit

Sub CATMain()

      MsgBox CATIA.Caption

End Sub
```

Save then run the macro by clicking the play icon, going to the run menu, or by pressing F5. A message box should pop-up displaying "CATIA V5". Click ok to end the program.

Workshop 2: Create Your Own VBA Modules and Classes

Complete Workshop 2 to learn more about creating macro libraries, creating modules, and message boxes.

WORKSHOP 2

Creating Your Own VBA Modules and Classes Tutorial

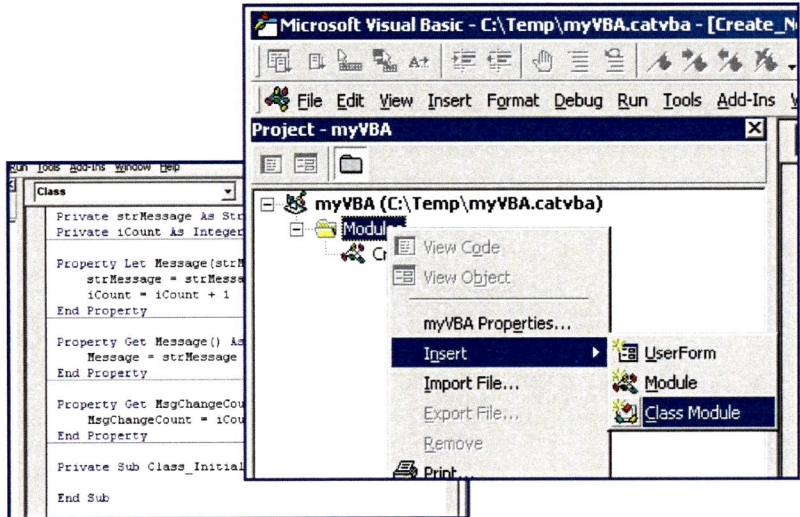

Workshop 2 – Introduction

■ Description

Although most of the CATIA VBA programming that you will do will involve the use of classes that are defined by the CATIA programming API, you will likely find it useful to define your own classes. In this workshop you will create a custom class in order to demonstrate the fundamentals of VBA object design.

■ Outline

1. Create a new class module in a new VBA library named "Messenger".
2. Give the Messenger class a simple "Public" property and use the class in a CATIA macro.
3. Enhance the Messenger class so that the "getting" and "setting" of its properties are controlled by "Get" and "Let" methods.
4. Give the Messenger class a method called "Capitalize" that serves to manipulate the string information that is stored in its properties.

Step 1

- Open the VBA editor by hitting Alt + F11. Create a new macro library and VBA project, called "myVBA".
- Double click on your newly created library (which will appear in Current Libraries).

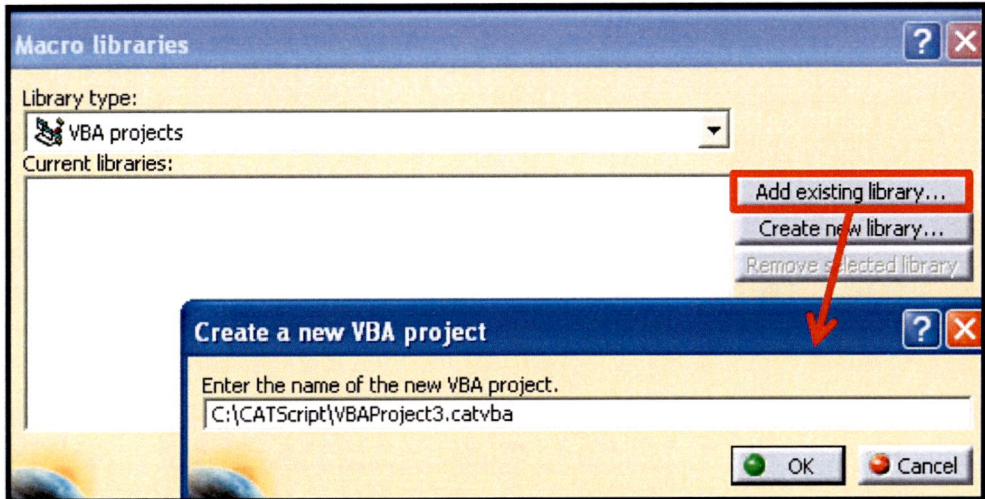

Step 2

•Ensure the project and properties boxes are visible by going to the top menu bar and clicking View >View Project Explorer and View Properties Window

•Right click on VBAProject (myVBA in this example) > Insert> Module.

•Use the (Name) field in the properties box to rename it "Create_New_Part_Document"

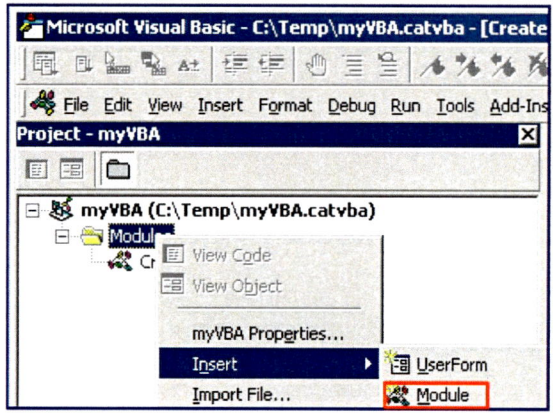 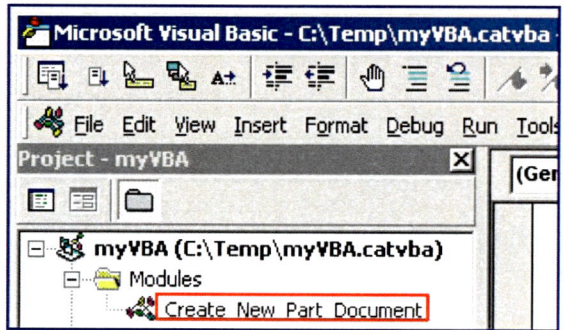

Step 3

Right click on the "Modules" folder of the VBA project and select Insert > Class Module.

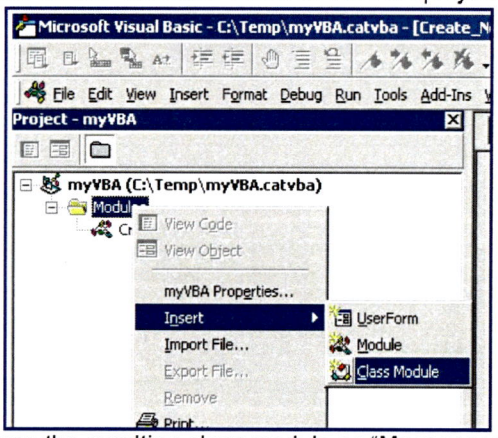 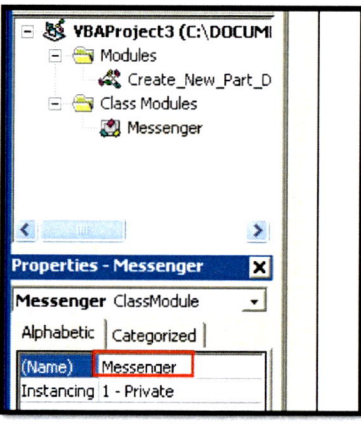

Rename the resulting class module as "Messenger" by clicking on Class1 then renaming the "Name" field in the properties box.

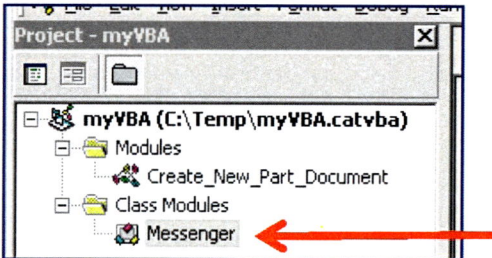

Step 4

- In the code window enter the line:

Public Message As String

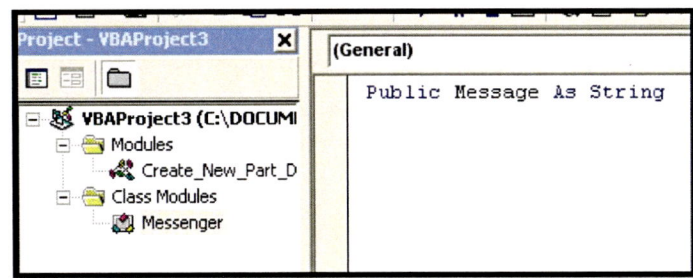

- Create another module on the VBA project. This needs to be a regular module, not a class module. Name it "UseTheMessenger".

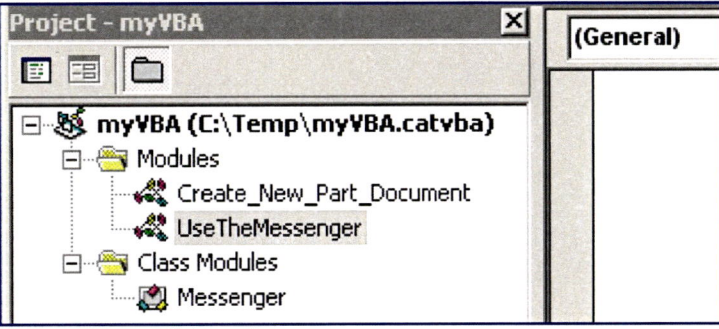

Step 5

Enter the code seen to the right into the "UseTheMessenger" module. Note the following:

- A Messenger object is dimmed. Because you created the class module named "Messenger" this class is immediately available in your VBA project.
- The "New" keyword orders the creation of a Messenger object. The variable "oMssgr" is set to this new object
- The property "Message" gets set to a specific value here.
- The Message property then gets used as it is passed to the message box.

Run the UseTheMessenger module by clicking the play button icon. A message box displaying "Hello" should result in your CATIA Window.

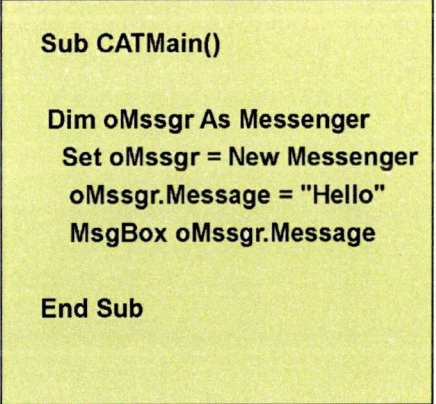

```
Sub CATMain()

Dim oMssgr As Messenger
Set oMssgr = New Messenger
oMssgr.Message = "Hello"
MsgBox oMssgr.Message


End Sub
```

Step 6

- Return to the code window for the class module "Messenger" and make the changes shown below. These changes have the effect of "hiding" the strMessage variable, but then create a read-only property named "Message" whose value is stored in the strMessage variable.

- Now go back to the "UseTheMessenger" module and make the changes shown below and to the right.

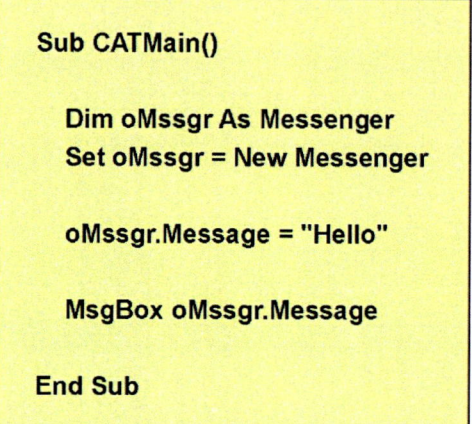

```
Private strMessage As String

Property Let Message(MessageIN As String)
   strMessage = MessageIN
End Property
```

```
Sub CATMain()

   Dim oMssgr As Messenger
   Set oMssgr = New Messenger

   oMssgr.Message = "Hello"

   MsgBox oMssgr.Message

End Sub
```

Step 7

Attempt to run "UseTheMessenger" and note that although the Message property can be "set", it fails when the property is "gotten". This is because no "Property Get" method has been defined (although, "Property Let" has been defined).

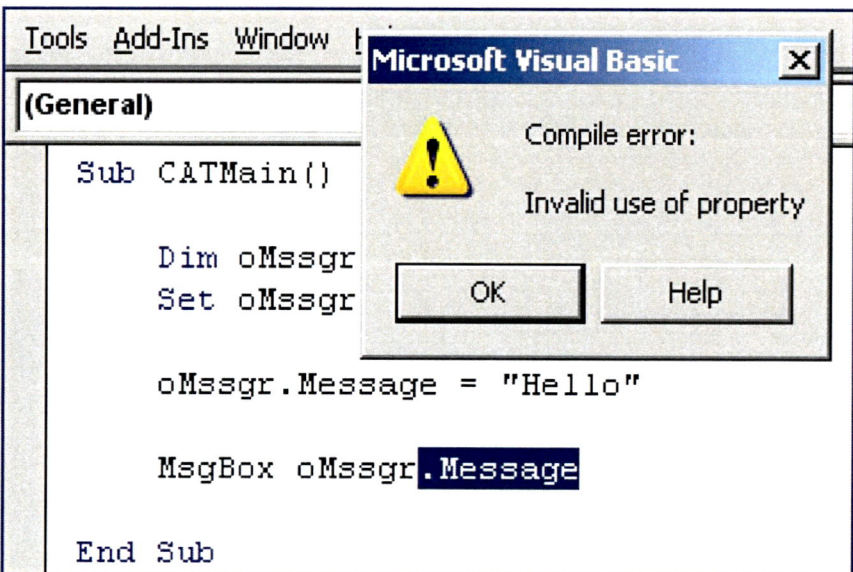

Step 8

- Return to the code window for the class module "Messenger" and add a "Property Get" method as shown below.
- Run the UseTheMessenger module again. It should work and the message "Hello" should be displayed.

Note: the advantage of strictly defining these "Let" and "Get" methods is that it gives the programmer control over whether a variable is read-only or read-write. Also, the code that is in the "Let" and "Get" methods can contain more complex operations and logic.

```
Private strMessage As String

Property Let Message(strMessageIN As String)
    strMessage = strMessageIN
End Property

Property Get Message() As String
    Message = strMessage
End Property
```

Step 9

Assume it would be desirable to keep count of how many times the Message property"s value is changed. To do this, create a private integer variable "iCount", change the "Property Let" method of the Message property, and add a "Property Get" method for a new property named "MsgChangeCount".

```
Private strMessage As String
Private iCount As Integer

Property Let Message(strMessageIN As String)
    strMessage = strMessageIN
    iCount = iCount + 1
End Property

Property Get Message() As String
    Message = strMessage
End Property

Property Get MsgChangeCount() As Integer
    MsgChangeCount = iCount
```

Step 10

- Change the "UseTheMessenger" module as shown below. Run it and a message should be displayed saying "Message changed 1 times".
- Change the "UseTheMessenger" module as shown to the lower right and run it again. A message should be displayed saying "Message changed 2 times".

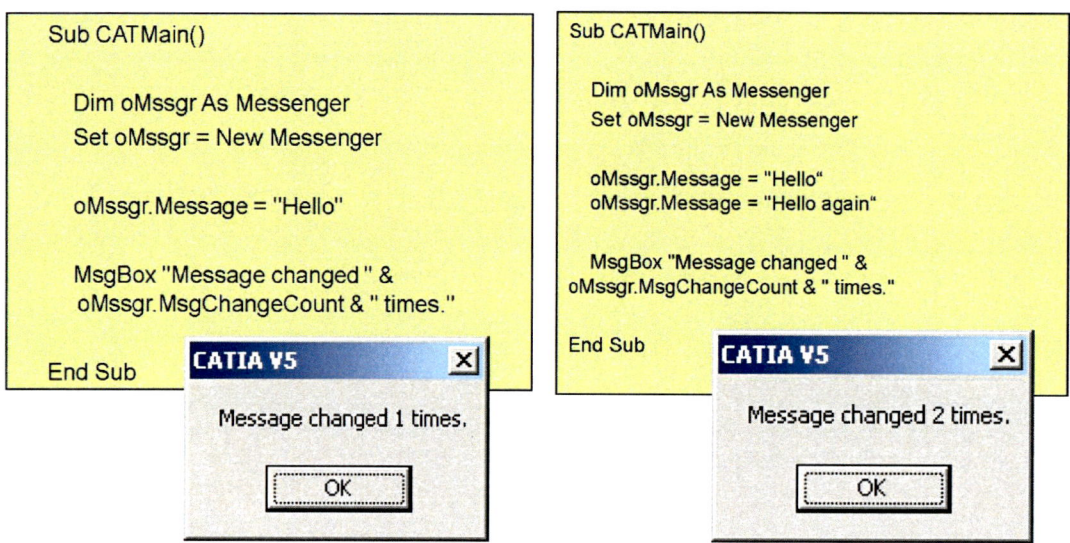

```
Sub CATMain()

    Dim oMssgr As Messenger
    Set oMssgr = New Messenger


    oMssgr.Message = "Hello"


    MsgBox "Message changed " & _
        oMssgr.MsgChangeCount & " times."


End Sub
```

CATIA V5

Message changed 1 times.

OK

```
Sub CATMain()

    Dim oMssgr As Messenger
    Set oMssgr = New Messenger

    oMssgr.Message = "Hello"
    oMssgr.Message = "Hello again"

    MsgBox "Message changed " & _
        oMssgr.MsgChangeCount & " times."

End Sub
```

CATIA V5

Message changed 2 times.

OK

Step 11

- Although the class works presently, there is one area where the class code could be more explicit. The "iCount" variable is incremented by one every time the Message property is changed, but it isn't clear what value iCount starts at. Testing the code has shown that it does start at zero, however it"s best to be explicit.

- In the code window for the Messenger class module, click the left drop-down menu and choose "Class".

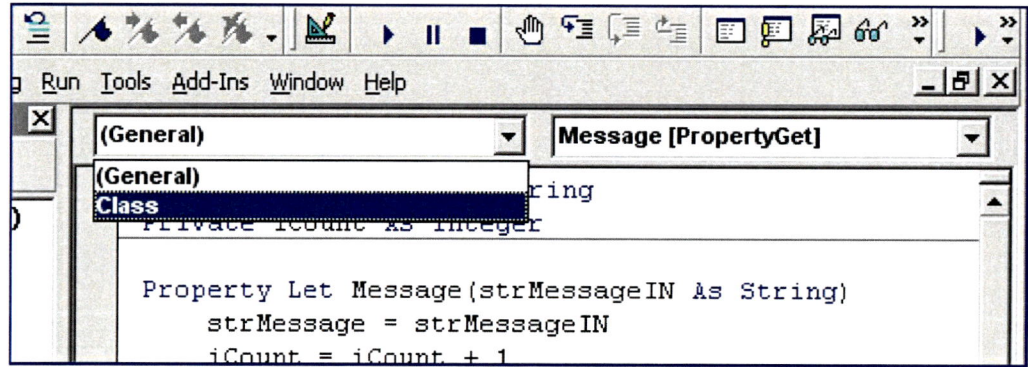

Step 12

The result of the previous step should be that the text for the subroutine "Class_Initialize" appears in the code window. Enter the code shown below into this sub. This has the effect of setting the value of the iCount to zero when a Messenger object is created with the "New" command.

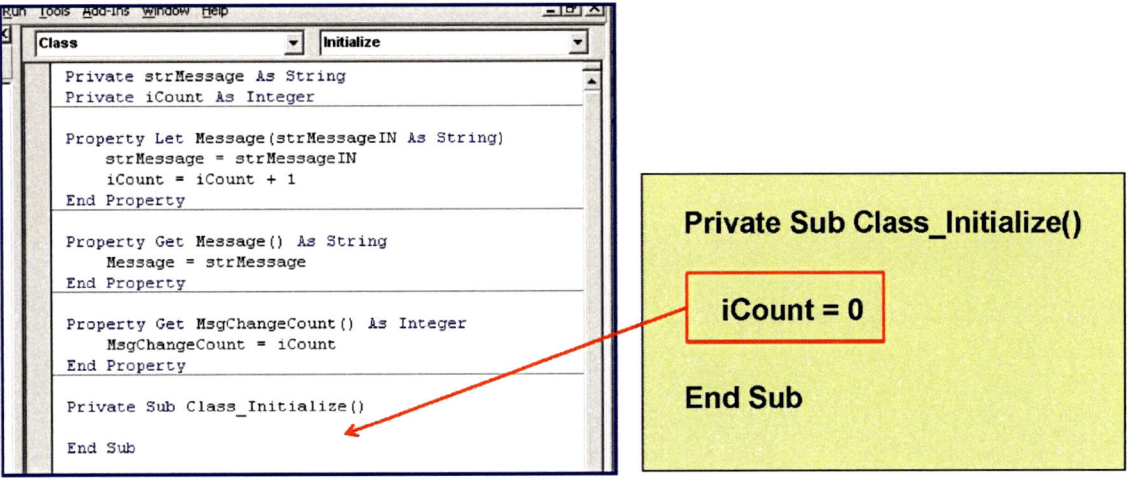

Step 13

- Properties have been defined for the messenger class. Now create a method for this class. This method will capitalize the message that is stored in the Message property. Enter the code seen below in the Messenger class module.

- The function "UCase" is a standard VBA function that takes a String as an argument and returns the same string in all capital letters.

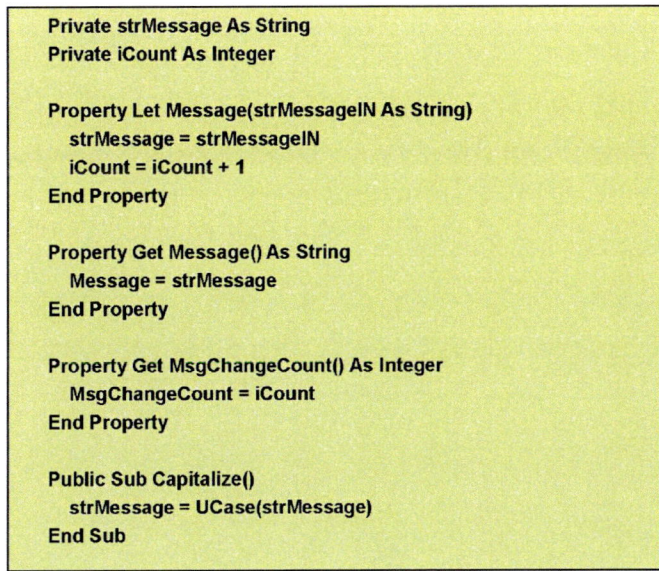

Step 14

- Change the "UseTheMessenger" code so that it calls this new capitalize method as shown.

- Run the code. Note that the capitalize method has the intended effect of changing the message box text from "Hello" to "HELLO".

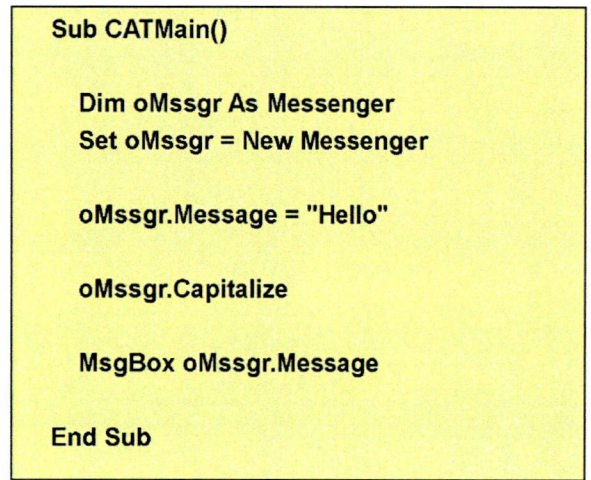

```
Sub CATMain()

    Dim oMssgr As Messenger
    Set oMssgr = New Messenger

    oMssgr.Message = "Hello"

    oMssgr.Capitalize

    MsgBox oMssgr.Message

End Sub
```

Workshop 2 – Conclusion

This concludes Workshop 2. In this workshop you have learned to:

•Create a VBA class

•Define a read-only property for the class (only provide a "Property Let" method)

•Define a read-write property for the class (provide both "Property Let" and "Property Get" methods

•Use the "Class_Initialize" subroutine to assign initial values to class variables

•Define a method for a class that operates on private variables of that class

Chapter 2: Programming Concepts

As stated earlier, CATIA utilizes object oriented programming, which came about due to the need to represent more complex ideas within a program. For example, you could say that a person is described by his height, weight, and hair color, and that every person has certain actions that they can perform, such as walking, eating, and sleeping. These "properties" and "methods" make up the "class" called "Person." Objects of this class can then be used in a program to represent individual people. Objects have properties that can be read or set as well as methods which modify their behavior.

Object - An entity (in CATIA or VB). Points, Pads, Parameters, etc. are all examples of CATIA objects. Objects use aggregation to denote a "consists of" relationship between objects. If object A consists of B and C this means object A aggregates B and C.

Property - Properties are characteristics of an object, like the object's name. Properties define the state of the Object during a specific moment. For example, the name of a PartDocument is a property of that object and is assessed by adding a period "." after the object's variable name, such as **oPartDoc.Name**.

Method - An action that an object can perform. Verbs are typically used for the names of Methods. For example, **oPartDoc.Save** is an action that the object can perform.

Collection - A group or list of similar objects which are put together for a specific reason. Collections are objects that aggregate an array of other objects.

Class - Class defines the type of Object. Inheritance is used to create hierarchies between classes and sub-classes.

Inheritance: Document, PartDocument, and ProductDocument are all classes but only PartDocument and ProductDocument are classes that inherit properties and methods from the Document class. This means they have all properties and methods in common which they inherit from the Document class but they also have their own properties and methods unique to themselves.

Dimming and Setting

Variables are "dimmed" (declared) as a type, either a "primitive" type (single, double, integer, string, etc.) or an object type (more complex). If you don't specify the type of variable VBA declares the variable as a Variant type which can accept any type of variable. In rare instances you'll have a good reason for using a Variant. But most of the time, you should use explicit variable types. One reason for doing so is that your code will run faster but the primary reason is that you'll reduce your coding errors due to the fact that:

(1) CATIA enforces the type of variable you specify.

(2). The second reason that it's always a good idea to declare your variable types explicitly is that it helps to document your intentions when you write code. This documentation is critical if you look at your code after several months have passed. Knowing whether a variable was intended to contain a number or text can make it much easier for you to read your old code, find errors, and then continue coding.

The "Dim" command is used to allocate a variable of any type. Primitive variables are populated with a value. Declaring variables with a 'Dim' statement helps save memory while running the program. If you have two variables declared as integers you could subtract or add them. But if you have two variables stored as names it wouldn't make sense to subtract them because that just doesn't mean anything! Declaring the type of variable allows you to make sense of what a variable can and cannot do.

Important note: In VB6 you need a separate line of code for every Dim statement (meaning you can't use `Dim w, h As String` it must be written as `Dim w As String: Dim h As String`).

After a variable is declared through dimming then it is "Set" or given a value. Do NOT use Set to assign a variable to an object property (`MyCamera3D.ViewPoint3D`) or an intrinsic type variable (`mystring = "directory"`) For object variables, the "Set" command is used to "point" the variable to the object. Within the program, the variable then represents that object unless it is "Set" to a different one.

The CATIA Object

The CATIA object is usually the first object that is referenced in any CATIA macro. This object represents the CATIA application itself, from which the macro is run. The CATIA object has many properties. For instance, it has a property called "FullName" which is a string. Another property is called "ActiveDocument". This property is an object itself, and even more specifically, it is a Document object.

The CATIA object is not dimmed or "declared" as it exists by default. The purpose of declaring and setting variables is to hold the properties of an object. Variables that hold objects require the "Set" keyword. The properties of objects can be accessed using the notation: Object.Property. Here is an object property example using the FullName property:

```
Option Explicit
Sub CATMain()
      Dim strFullName as String
      strFullName = CATIA.FullName
      Dim doc1 as Document
      Set doc1=CATIA.ActiveDocument
End Sub
```

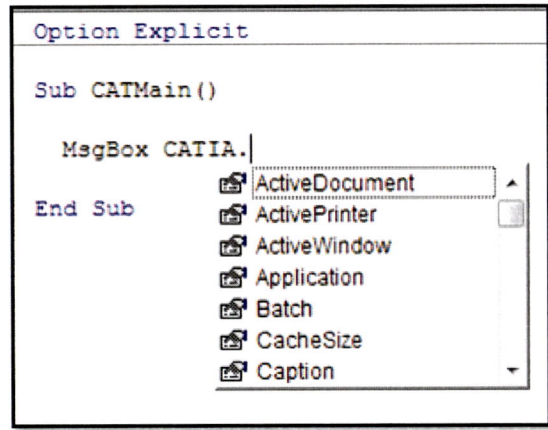

The Document object has a string property called "FullName", which returns the file path of the document. You can "grab" the FullName property and display its value or you can access this property more directly, as shown in the following examples.

Remember, a single quotation is used to display comments or notes which will be used to help explain each code step-by-step. It's a good idea to add comments to your own code to help you remember what your thought process was or in case another user needs to edit your code they won't be completely lost. In other words, the comments in your code should read like a book, telling the story of what the code does.

Option 1:

```
'Display the file path name in a message box
Sub CATMain()
      Dim doc1 as Document
      Set doc1 = CATIA.ActiveDocument
      MsgBox doc1.FullName
End Sub
```

Option 2:

```
'use a "chain" of property references

Sub CATMain()

    'Display a message box with the full name of the document
    MsgBox CATIA.ActiveDocument.FullName
    'Display a message box with the number of selections in the document
    MsgBox CATIA.ActiveDocument.Selection.Count

End Sub
```

Message Boxes

The **MsgBox** function in VBA displays a message box in a window and waits for a user to click on a button. Message boxes are frequently used to display strings to users while running a program. Message boxes are helpful debugging tools to insert into code to display what a variable is currently set to. There are multiple options for the types of buttons displayed on the message box pop-up window.

Type of MsgBox Buttons		
0	vbOKOnly	OK button only
1	vbOKCancel	OK and Cancel buttons
2	vbAbortRetryIgnore	Abort, Retry, and Ignore buttons
3	vbYesNoCancel	Yes, No, and Cancel buttons
4	vbYesNo	Yes and No buttons
5	vbRetryCancel	Retry and Cancel buttons

To ask a question with a message box use this syntax:

Value = MsgBox (message, [parameter], [Title])

```
Option Explicit

Sub CATMain()

  MsgBox CATIA.Caption
  Msgbox ("Click yes or no, vbYesNo,
    MsgBox(Prompt, [Buttons As VbMsgBoxStyle = vbOKOnly], [Title], [HelpFile], [Context]) As VbMsgBoxResult
End Sub
```

```
Dim Response As Integer
```

```
Response = MsgBox("Are you sure you want to quit?", vbYesNo, "Confirm to Quit")

     If Response = vbYes Then

     End 'ends the program

End If
```

Input Boxes

The message box approach only allows for pre-determined responses. To drive a program event, you may want to ask a user to input data such as text, numbers, or a formula. In this case, an input box is the answer. Input box syntax is:

value = Inputbox(message, title, value)

```
dimensionOne=Inputbox("Please   enter   the   first   dimension   :",   "Enter   the_
Dimension", 0)
```

There are a few potential issues when using an input box. When a user hits cancel the inputbox function returns an empty string. Another possible problem with an input box is that it might return the wrong type of data, like if the code is expecting a number and a user enters text string. Use error handling (discussed later) to avoid these potential pitfalls.

Parameter Input Box

CATIA macros can have input parameters. This means when the macro is run a dialog box is immediately opened allowing the user to enter input values. The syntax is: Sub CATMain(Parameter 1, Parameter2,...) where the parameters might be a string, integer, double, sketch, pad, etc.. Sub CATMain(Length, Width)

Workshop 3: Creating a Basic VBA Program from Scratch
Practice creating a VBA program from scratch with Workshop 3.

WORKSHOP 3

Creating a Basic VBA Program from Scratch

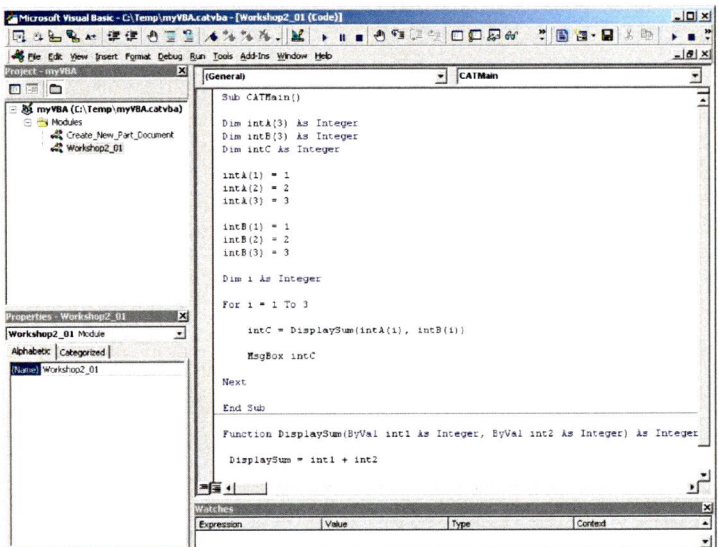

Workshop 3 – Introduction

■ Description

In this workshop, as opposed to starting a CATIA VBA program by recording a macro, you will instead insert a new module into an existing CATIA VBA library and type the program statements in manually. You will also see the difference between Subs and Functions, and get experience using "primitive" variable types, arrays, and For loops.

■ Outline

1. Create a new module in the macro library created in Workshop 2 called myVBA_01

2. Program a routine that creates two integer variables, adds them, and then displays the result in a "message box".

3. Create a new module with a routine using a Sub

4. Create a new module with a routine using a Function

5. Create a new module with a routine using arrays and a For loop.

Step 1: Create a new module named Workshop2_01

- Right-click on the myVBA project on the Project tree and select **Insert** > **Module**.
- Rename the newly created module "Workshop2_01"

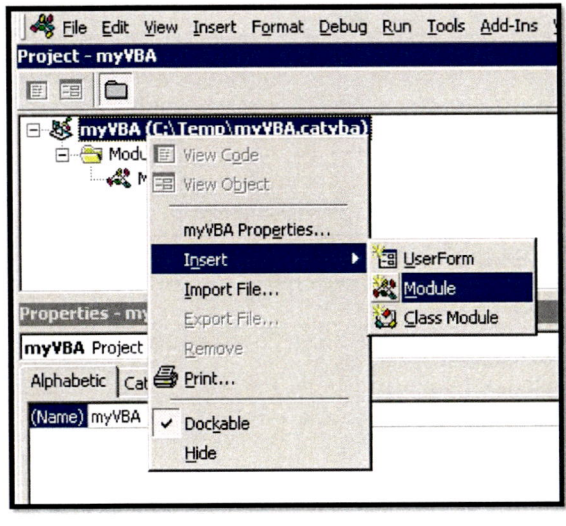
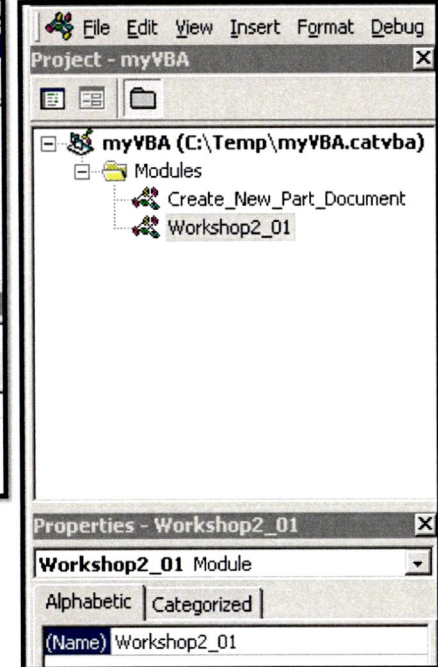

Step 2

- In the code window, type the code shown below
- Click **Save** on the **File** menu to save the your changes.

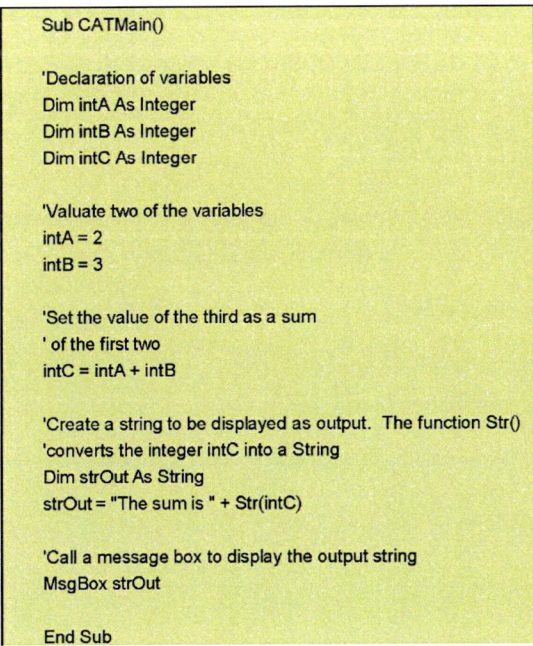
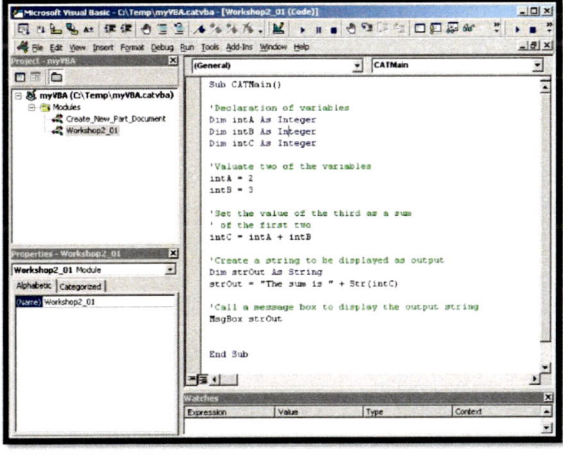

```
Sub CATMain()

'Declaration of variables
Dim intA As Integer
Dim intB As Integer
Dim intC As Integer

'Valuate two of the variables
intA = 2
intB = 3

'Set the value of the third as a sum
' of the first two
intC = intA + intB

'Create a string to be displayed as output.  The function Str()
'converts the integer intC into a String
Dim strOut As String
strOut = "The sum is " + Str(intC)

'Call a message box to display the output string
MsgBox strOut

End Sub
```

Step 3

- Close the VBA editor.
- Open the Macros menu through **Tools > Macro > Macros**.
- Select the **WorkShop2_01** macro on the list and click the Run button
- Note that the value "5" is displayed in the message box.

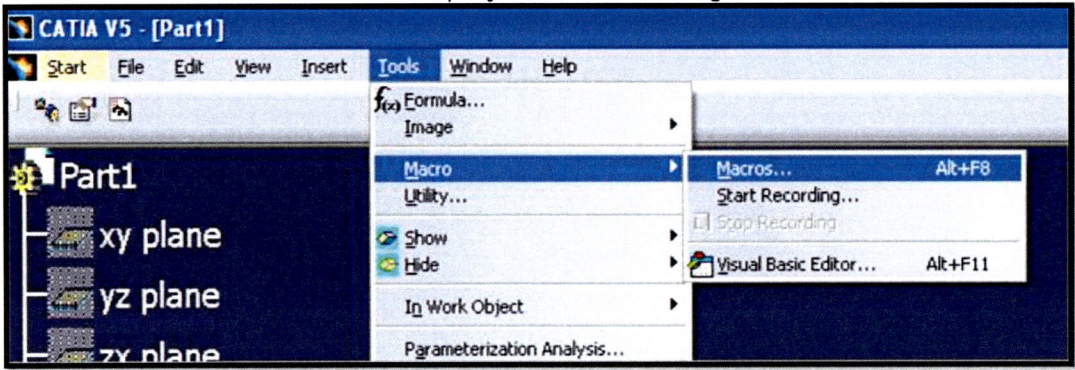

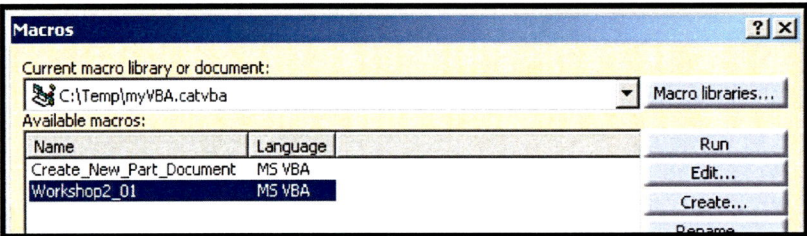

Step 4

- Right-click on the myVBA project on the Project tree and select **Insert > Module**.
- Rename the newly created module "Workshop2_02".
- In the code window, type the code shown below.

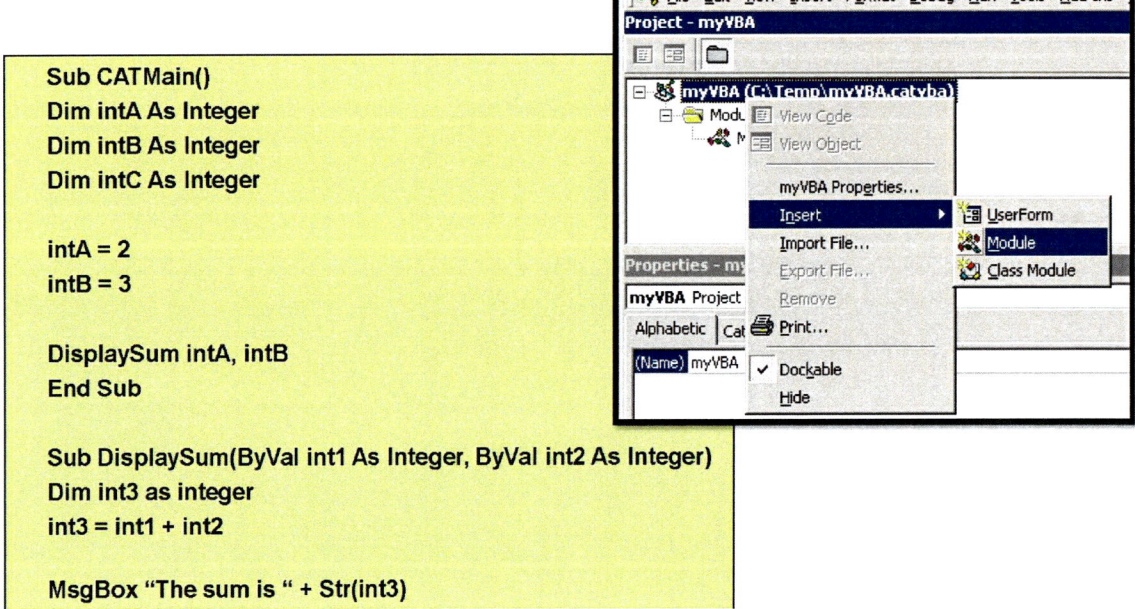

```
Sub CATMain()
Dim intA As Integer
Dim intB As Integer
Dim intC As Integer

intA = 2
intB = 3

DisplaySum intA, intB
End Sub

Sub DisplaySum(ByVal int1 As Integer, ByVal int2 As Integer)
Dim int3 as integer
int3 = int1 + int2

MsgBox "The sum is " + Str(int3)
```

Step 5

- Click **Save** on the **File** menu to save the your changes.
- Run the macro, this time by using the "Run" button in the VBA editor. This requires that the cursor in the code window is sitting within the "CATMain" Sub.

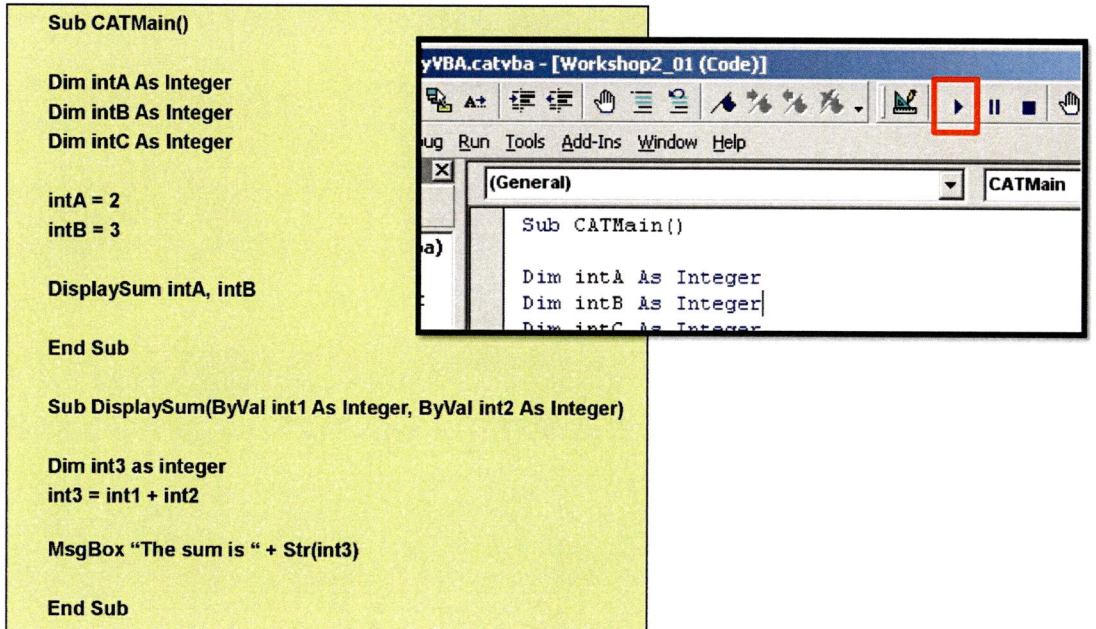

```
Sub CATMain()

Dim intA As Integer
Dim intB As Integer
Dim intC As Integer

intA = 2
intB = 3

DisplaySum intA, intB

End Sub

Sub DisplaySum(ByVal int1 As Integer, ByVal int2 As Integer)

Dim int3 as integer
int3 = int1 + int2

MsgBox "The sum is " + Str(int3)

End Sub
```

Step 6

- Right-click on the myVBA project on the Project tree and select **Insert** > **Module**.
- Rename the newly created module "Workshop2_03"
- In the code window, type the code shown below
- Click **Save** on the **File** menu to save the your changes.
- Run the macro, this time by using the "Run" button in the VBA editor. This requires that the cursor in the code window is sitting within the "CATMain" Sub.

```
Sub CATMain()
Dim intA As Integer
Dim intB As Integer
Dim intC As Integer

intA = 2
intB = 3

intC = DisplaySum(intA, intB)

MsgBox "The sum is " + Str(intC)
End Sub

Function DisplaySum(ByVal int1 As Integer, ByVal int2 As Integer) As Integer
```

Step 7

- Right-click on the myVBA project on the Project tree and select **Insert** > **Module**.

- Rename the newly created module "Workshop2_04"

- In the code window, type the code shown to the right

- Click **Save** on the **File** menu to save the your changes.

- Run the macro.

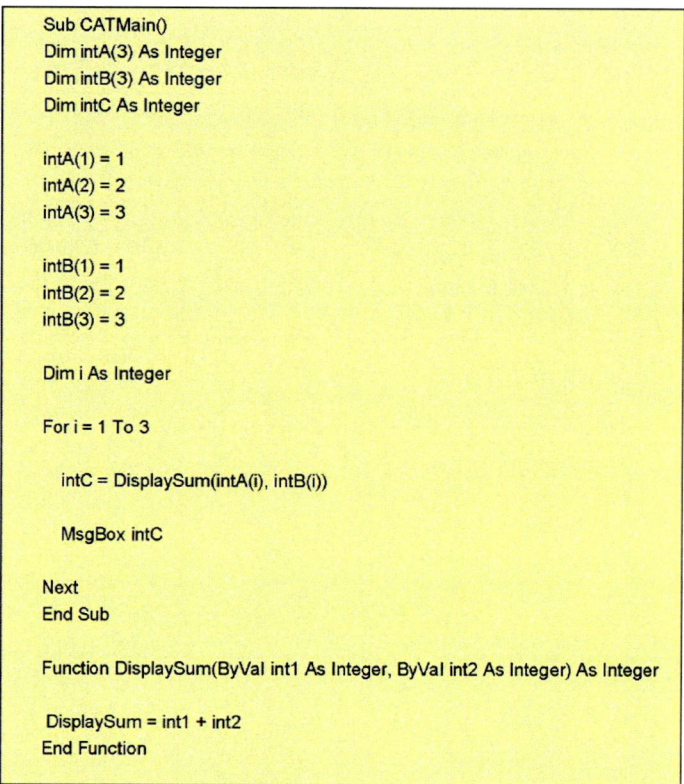

```
Sub CATMain()
Dim intA(3) As Integer
Dim intB(3) As Integer
Dim intC As Integer

intA(1) = 1
intA(2) = 2
intA(3) = 3

intB(1) = 1
intB(2) = 2
intB(3) = 3

Dim i As Integer

For i = 1 To 3

    intC = DisplaySum(intA(i), intB(i))

    MsgBox intC

Next
End Sub

Function DisplaySum(ByVal int1 As Integer, ByVal int2 As Integer) As Integer

DisplaySum = int1 + int2
End Function
```

Workshop 3 – Conclusion

This concludes Workshop 3. In this workshop you have learned to:

- Create a CATIA VBA program from scratch

- Use "primitive" variable types such as integers and strings

- Use a Sub (subroutine) to encapsulate code that is to be called multiple times throughout a program

- Use a Function in a way similar to a Sub, but when a return value is desired

- Use an array to store a list of primitives (integers in this case) and then iterate through that array using a For loop

Chapter 3: Documents and Windows

There are three main CATIA objects: Document, PartDocument, and ProductDocument. All three are classes, but both PartDocument and ProductDocument are classes that inherit properties and methods from the Document class. Therefore, the PartDocument and ProductDocument class have in common all the properties and methods that they inherit from the Document class, but they each have their own unique properties and methods as well. The specification tree of a part document roughly corresponds to the underlying programmatic structure of the part object, but not exactly.

There are three main types of Documents: PartDocument, ProductDocument, and DrawingDocument. To create a new part, product, or drawing document:

```
Dim myDoc as Document
Set myDoc = CATIA.Documents.Add("Part")
Set myDoc=CATIA.Documents.Add("Product")
Set myDoc=CATIA.Documents.Add("Drawing")
```

```
Option Explicit

Sub CATMain()

Dim myDoc As Document
Set myDoc = CATIA.Documents.Add(
                          Add(docType As String) As Document

End Sub
```

Likewise, a part, product, or drawing already created and saved in a folder or directory can be added by:

```
Dim myDoc as Document
Set myDoc=CATIA.Documents.Open("C:\MyDocuments\MyPart.CATPart")
```

Documents

There are two main collections aggregated under the CATIA application object: Documents and Windows. In this chapter, we'll discuss documents and later on we'll look at Windows.

Documents - There are many types of documents that are used in V5: CATPart, CATProduct, CATProcess, CATDrawing, CATAnalysis, etc. These are all housed in the Documents collection and they contain all geometry, process, and product information. The Document object is an abstract object. Collections are lists of objects. The CATIA collection index starts at 1 (not 0). The Documents collection contains several methods including:

- **Add:** create a new document. Objects can be added to a collection using the "add" method: `Set myNewPart = CATIA.Documents.Add("Part")`
- **Open:** open an already created document
- **NewFrom:** create a new document from another file
- **Item:** Get a specific document from the documents collection. Item allows programmers to navigate through items by name: Item("PartBody") or by Index: Item(1). However, if there is no item named, such as no Body named PartBody in your part then the program will fail. Every part has a body in it so using Item(1) would be more robust and won't fail.

A method is an action taking place on an object. Saving an object is a method. Each Document can then be manipulated by several different methods:

- **Activate:** activate the document
- **Save:** saves the document
- **SaveAs:** save the document to a specified file
- **Close:** close the document

CATProducts in CATIA V5 match up with the object type in VB called the ProductDocument. This is the root object for all development having to do with assemblies. What confuses most people when they start working with the Product Object Model is the fact that every "Product" has a collection of "Products" underneath it. The Root product has a collection of products. Each Product in the collection has its own collection of Products. This structure of *Product.Products.Item(1).Products.Item(1)…* can go multiple levels deep. The concept is fairly easy though- each product in the tree has a collection of products under it. The collection may be empty (i.e. count=0), but it does exist.

The "Products" collection is just like any other collection. You can see how many products are in a sub-assembly using "Count":

```
intNumberOfParts = objProductCollection.Count
```

You can get a specific item of the collection using "Item":

```
Set myProduct = objProductCollection.Item(3)
```

To get the Product Document:

```
Dim objProductDoc As ProductDocument
Set objProductDoc = CATIA.ActiveDocument
```

Get the Root Product from the Product document:

```
Dim objRootProduct As Product
Set objRootProduct = objProductDoc.Product
```

Get the collection of level1 products:

```
Dim objProductCollection As Products
Set objProductCollection = objRootProduct.Products
```

Subroutines and Functions

Subroutines and functions are good for encapsulating code that needs to be called repeatedly. Functions "return" a value, subroutines do not. Arguments may be passed in as "ByRef" or "ByVal" (ByVal is the default). The following code is another example of how to display a "Hello" message box using multiple sub statements.

```
Sub CATMain()

    Dim strMessage as String
    CallMe strMessage
        MsgBox strMessage

End Sub

Sub Callme(ByRef strMsg As String)
    strMsg = "Hello"
End Sub
```

Save and SaveAs

The Document object includes the "Save" and "Save As" methods. The "Save" method takes no arguments and returns nothing.

```
CATIA.ActiveDocument.Save
```

The "Save As" method takes a string as an argument but returns nothing

```
Dim doc1 as Document
Set doc1 = CATIA.ActiveDocument
doc1.SaveAs "C:\Example.CATPart"
```

Another option is to use the FileSelectionBox method to prompt the user to select the file name and folder:

```
Dim strFilePath As String  'no set because it's a string
strFilePath=CATIA.FileSelectionBox("Save    the    part:",    "*.CATPart",_
CATFileSelectionModeSave)
doc1.SaveAs strFilePath
```

Open a Product

An additional line of code is needed to open a product versus saving one using the FileSelectionBox method.

```
Dim strFilePath As String
strFilePath=CATIA.FileSelectionBox("Enter   part   number",   "*.CATProduct",_
CATFileSelectionModeOpen)
Dim oProductDoc As ProductDocument
Set oProductDoc = CATIA.Documents.Open(strFilePath)
```

Get Workbench

The Document object also has methods such as the "GetWorkbench" method. The GetWorkbench command takes a string as an argument and returns a Workbench object. To load the structural workbench:

```
Dim doc1 as Document
Set doc1 = CATIA.ActiveDocument
Dim workbench1 as Workbench
Set workbench1 =doc1.GetWorkbench("Structural")
```

Working with Collections: Count and Item

Collections are special kinds of objects that hold a list of objects of a certain class. The property "Count" and the method "Item()" are frequently used on collections in CATIA. For example:

```
Sub CATMain()
    'Count the number of open documents
    Dim docs1 as Documents
    Set docs1 = CATIA.Documents

MsgBox "The number of open documents is " & docs1.Count
'Accessing the first Document object in the collection

    Dim doc1 as Document
    Set doc1 = docs1.Item(1)

MsgBox "The FullName of the first document is " & doc1.FullName
End Sub
```

Windows

A **window** is an abstract object that falls under the Windows collection. The Windows collection contains information about how the data from the documents collection will be seen in the CATIA window. It controls items such as:

- Are the parts shaded or wireframe?
- What orientation is the part being viewed in?
- How close or far away is the zoom level on the part?
- What color is the background screen?

Everything in this collection has to do with HOW the data is seen. The ActiveWindow property is the current active window. CATIA models are displayed according to specific viewpoints and options called a Viewer. Viewer methods include:

- **Translate:** applies a translation
- **Rotate:** applies a rotation
- **Reframe:** fits the model all in the window and centers on it
- **Update:** updates the current viewer contents
- **ZoomIn/ZoomOut:** zooms in or out on the model
- **CaptureToFile:** used to take a screen capture

Windows is the CATIA object that displays documents in a viewable 2D or 3D form. The **Activate method** is used to make a window become active and also implies the documents displayed in the active window are also active.

```
Sub CATMain()

'set the current document as the active document
Dim Doc
Set Doc = CATIA.ActiveDocument

'set the current window as the active window
Set WindCol = CATIA.Windows

'count the number of open windows
Dim DocNum
DocNum = WindCol.Count

'declare the active window variable
Dim ActWin

'create a new CATPart
Dim part2
Set part2 = CATIA.Documents.Add("CATPart")

'rename the new part
part2.Product.PartNumber = "My New Part"

'There are two ways to change the active window: using the index number or by
name

'return the second window in the collection
Set ActWin = CATIA.Windows.Item(2)

'return the window named "Enovia V6"
'Set ActWin = CATIA.Windows.item("ENOVIAV6.CATProduct")

'activate the window
ActWin.Activate

End Sub
```

Windows can also be arranged using the Arrange method. To arrange the open windows in a cascade style:

```
CATIA.Windows.Arrange(catArrangeCascade)
```

```
Other Arrange methods include catArrangeTiledHorizontal and
catArrangeTiledVertical.
```

Viewer Commands

Just to help avoid confusion, the Viewers collection enables the window to display the application data in the desired mode using viewers. The SpecsAndGeomWindow object features a viewer and a specification tree viewer. There are a few steps and methods to change the viewpoint of a CATIA document. The object "SpecsAndGeomWindow" contains a 2 or 3D viewer as well as a specification tree viewer. First, access the 3D viewer from the current CATIA window:

```
Dim objViewer3D As Viewer3D
Set objViewer3D = CATIA.ActiveWindow.ActiveViewer
```

Next, we need to access one of the "Camera" objects from the current document. A camera object is a static version of the window viewer object:

```
Dim objCamera3D As Camera3D
Set objCamera3D=objCATIA.ActiveDocument.Cameras.Item(1)
```

Unlike CATIA V4, in V5 the views (or Cameras) for a particular document are saved in that document. So, to change the view of a document we need to set the 3DViewer viewpoint to the Camera viewpoint:

```
objViewer3D.Viewpoint3D = Camera3D.Viewpoint3D
```

Once you access the ActiveViewer of the current window you can also control many other display properties:

```
Dim objViewer As Viewer3D
Set objViewer = CATIA.ActiveWindow.ActiveViewer

'Translate the view
objViewer.Translate(translationVector)

'Rotate the view:
objViewer.Rotate(axisOfRotation, rotationAngle)

'Create a new view or camera
objViewer.NewCamera()

'To reframe a window
objViewer.Reframe()
```

```
'To Zoom In
objViewer.ZoomIn()

'To Zoom Out
objViewer.ZoomOut()
```

To turn off the specification tree:

```
Dim objSpecWindow As SpecsAndGeomWindow
Set objSpecWindow = CATIA.ActiveWindow
objSpecWindow.Layout = WindowGeomOnly
```

This shows both the spec tree and the geometry WindowSpecsAndGeom:

```
'This shuts off the geometry and shows only the spec tree
WindowSpecsOnly

'to make the window occupy the whole screen

objSpecWindow.WindowState = catWindowStateMaximized
```

The size of the active window can also be adjusted.

```
Dim myView As Viewer
Set myView = CATIA.ActiveWindow.ActiveViewer

Dim h As String
Dim w As String
H=myView.Height
W=myView.Width
myView.Reframe
```

Part Object

All the geometrical data including part bodies, geometrical sets, sketches, solid features, surfaces, etc. are found in the Part object. The spec tree of a part document roughly corresponds to the underlying structure of the Part object. Objects include product, bodies, sketches, and hybridbodies.

To update a part use the update function:

```
Dim part1As Part
Set part1 = partDocument1.part
Part1.Update
```

Product Object

Information in the properties dialog box for a CATPart including the part number, revision number, description, definition, and nomenclature is found in the Product object.

Here is a twofold example: (1) How to change the PartNumber and (2) the difference between recording a macro and writing code by hand.

```
'using the macro recorder you would get this
Dim oProd As Product
Set oProd=oPartDoc.Product
oProd.Name="New Part Number"

'you can replace the lines of code above with the following
oPartDoc.Product.PartNumber="New Part Number"
```

Bodies Collection

Under the Part is the Bodies collection which contains the Body objects. New CATparts always contain at least one body (typically called named "PartBody"). Bodies are active using the InWorkObject property of the Part object. Methods of the Bodies collection include:

- Add: create a new body
- Item: get a body from the collection by index number or name

To rename the part body from "PartBody" to "Main Part Body":

```
Set oPB=oPartDoc.Part.Bodies.Item(1).Name="Main Part Body"
```

After the new body is created use the Update method to update the part:

```
oPart.Update
```

Geometrical Sets

In CATIA V5 VBA automation, Geometrical Sets are called Hybrid Bodies. The primary methods of HybridBodies are Add and Item. Newly created parts do not contain any geometrical sets. Use the Add method of the HydridBodies object to create a new geometrical set and rename it, like so:

```
'this is a CATScript, active document is a part
Dim oPrt As PartDocuments
Set oPrt=CATIA.ActiveDocument.Part
Dim oGeom As HybridBody
Set oGeom = oPrt.HybridBodies.Add
oGeom.Name = "New Geo Set"
```

To make the newly created geometrical set the in work object:

```
oPrt.InWorkObject = oGeom
```

Features like points and splines are added to the geometrical set through the AppendHybridShape method.

```
oHB.AppendHybridShape oFill
```

Another example: create an intersection between and extrude and a fill:

```
Dim oInt As HybridShapeIntersection
Set oInt=oHF.AddNewIntersection(oExtrude, oFill)
oGS.AppendHybridShape oInt
```

We'll learn about deleting and copying geometrical sets after learning about Selection.

Loops

Looping is often used to perform iterative actions. Just like any other part of CATIA, there are multiple methods to accomplish the same task. There are essentially three types of loop that you can write in Visual Basic for Applications:

- Use **FOR ... NEXT** when you want to loop a given number of times.
- Use **DO UNTIL ... LOOP** when you want to loop *until* a condition is true, or the very similar **DO WHILE ... LOOP** when you want to loop *while* a condition is true.
- Use **FOR EACH ... NEXT** when you want to loop over the objects in a collection.

Syntax of a For...Next loop is:

```
For a_counter = start_counter To end_counter
'Perform action
Next a_counter
```

a_counter is the time keeper element of the loop. Start_counter is the beginning value of the loop and will perform the actions within the loop until the counter reached the end_counter value.

Method 1: For Each Loop

```
Sub CATMain()

      Dim documents1 as Documents
      Set documents1 = CATIA.Documents
      Dim doc1 as Document

            For Each doc1 in documents1

            MsgBox doc1.Name

            Next

End Sub
```

Method 2: For...Next Loop

```
Sub CATMain()

      Dim documents1 as Documents
      Set documents1 = CATIA.Documents
      Dim doc1 as Document

Dim i As Integer
For i = 1 To CATIA.Documents.Count

Set doc1 = CATIA.Documents.Item(i)
MsgBox doc1.Name

Next
End Sub
```

Do While Loop syntax:

```
'loop while a condition is true
Do [{While | Until} condition]
[statements]
[Exit Do]
[statements]
Loop
```

Workshop 4: Objects in CATIA VBA
Learn more about eh object browser, properties of objects, methods, and documents in Workshop 4.

WORKSHOP 4

Objects in CATIA VBA

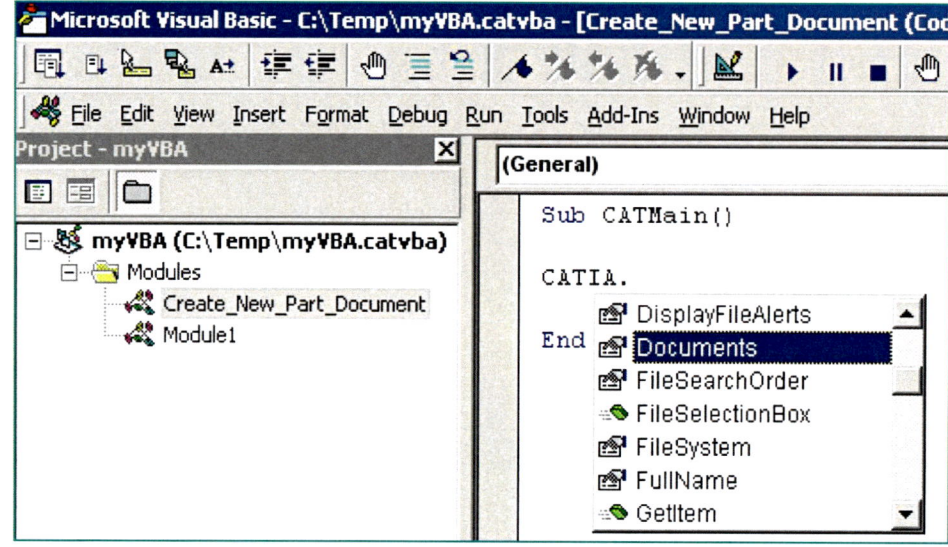

Workshop 4 – Introduction

■ Description

In this workshop you will explore the basics of objects, their properties, and their methods in CATIA VBA programming. You will also learn how to use the CATIA object browser documentation.

■ Outline

1. Create a new module in the macro library myVBA_01.
2. Start an "empty" CATMain() Sub.
3. Observe the properties and methods of the CATIA object.
4. Grab the Documents collection and display its Count property.

Workshop 4 – Introduction

■ Description

In this workshop you will explore the basics of objects, their properties, and their methods in CATIA VBA programming. You will also learn how to use the CATIA object browser documentation.

■ Outline

1. Create a new module in the macro library myVBA_01.
2. Start an "empty" CATMain() Sub.
3. Observe the properties and methods of the CATIA object.
4. Grab the Documents collection and display its Count property.

Step 1

- Create a new module in the myVBA macro library called "CATIAbasicObjects"

- In the code window type "Sub CATMain()" and hit Enter.

- In the CATMain() Sub, type "CATIA." (notice the period) and note that the "Intellisense" drop-down appears, displaying a list of properties and methods of the CATIA object.

- Note that the "Documents" property of the CATIA object is on the list. This is what is depicted in the CATIA object model diagram below.

NOTE: the object called "Application" is the same as the CATIA object in the VBA view.

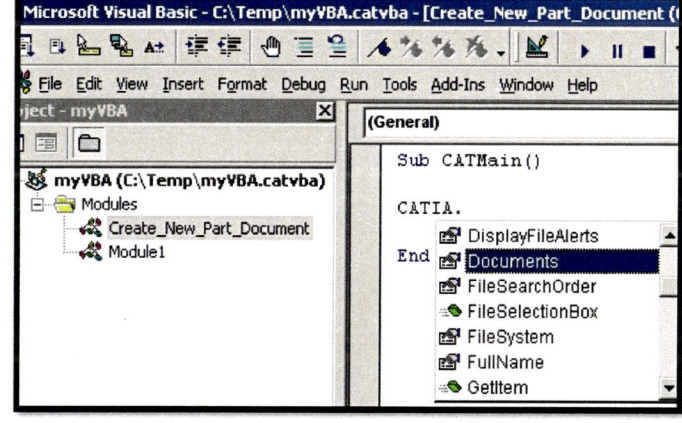

61

Step 2

- Scroll down the Intellisense drop-down and note that the "Windows" property is there as well.
- So "Documents" and "Windows" are both properties of the CATIA object, but they are also objects themselves. Moreover, they are a special type of object: they are collections.
- Erase the text "CATIA." that you just entered.

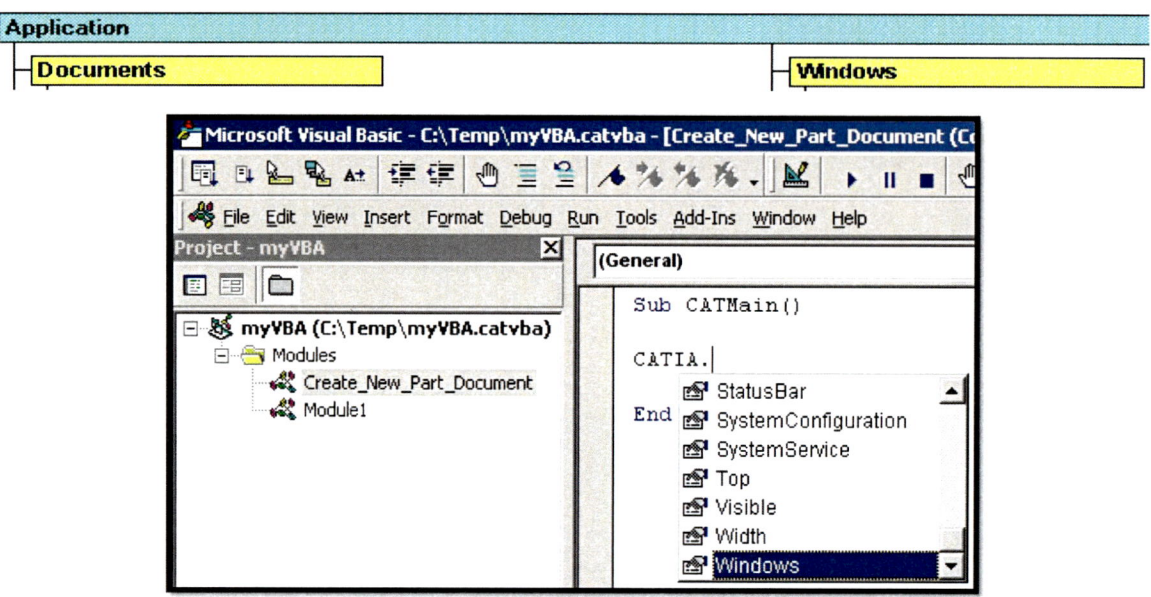

Step 3

- Open 3 new parts in CATIA, accepting their default names and save them anywhere on disk.
- Enter the code below into the code window.
- Run the macro using the "Run" button. The count of open documents should be displayed.

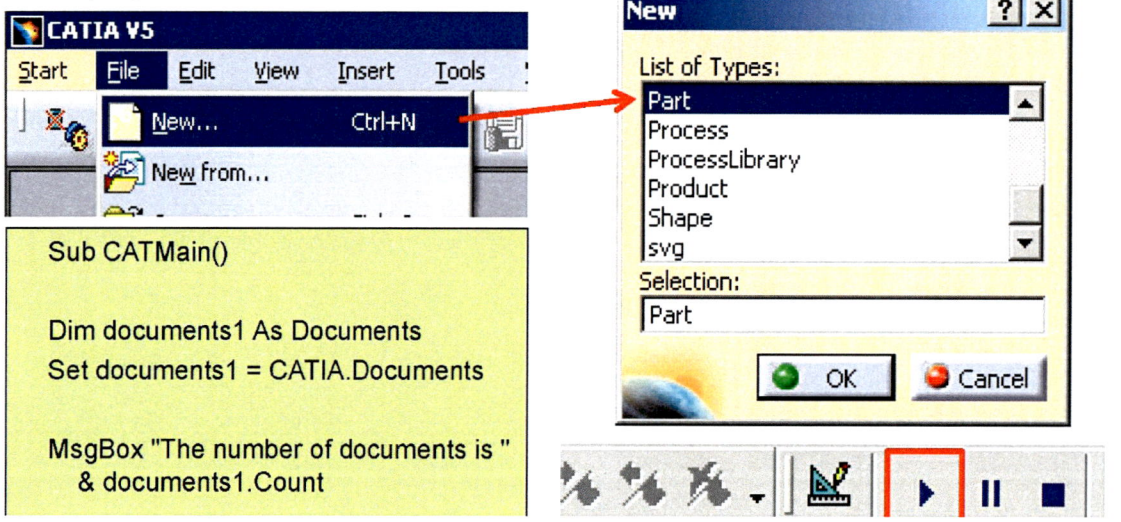

```
Sub CATMain()

Dim documents1 As Documents
Set documents1 = CATIA.Documents

MsgBox "The number of documents is "
    & documents1.Count
```

Step 4

Add the code shown below and re-run the macro:

Note: The method Item() was used on the Documents object "documents1" in order to retrieve a member of the collection. Then the "Name" property and "FullName" property of the Document object "doc1" were used. These properties return Strings, which were displayed in the message boxes.

```
Sub CATMain()

Dim documents1 As Documents
Set documents1 = CATIA.Documents

MsgBox "The number of documents is " & documents1.Count

Dim doc1 As Document
Set doc1 = documents1.Item(1)

MsgBox doc1.Name
MsgBox doc1.FullName

End Sub
```

Step 5

- Modify the previous code as shown in the code window to the right

- Run the new code using the "Run" button.

Note that the "For each" loop iterates through the Documents collection "documents1". The same effect could be achieved with the below code, but a "For Each" loop is simpler:

```
Dim doc1 As Document
Dim i as Integer

For i = 1 to documents1.Count

    Set doc1 = documents1.Item(i)
    MsgBox doc1.Name
```

```
Sub CATMain()

Dim documents1 As Documents
Set documents1 = CATIA.Documents

MsgBox "The number of documents is " &
    documents1.Count

Dim doc1 As Document
'Set doc1 = documents1.Item(1)

'MsgBox doc1.Name
'MsgBox doc1.FullName

For Each doc1 in documents1

    MsgBox doc1.Name

Next
```

Step 6

Modify the previous code as shown in the code window to the right:

1) Uncomment a couple lines
2) Comment the "For Each" loop out completely
3) Add more code

Run the new code using the "Run" button.

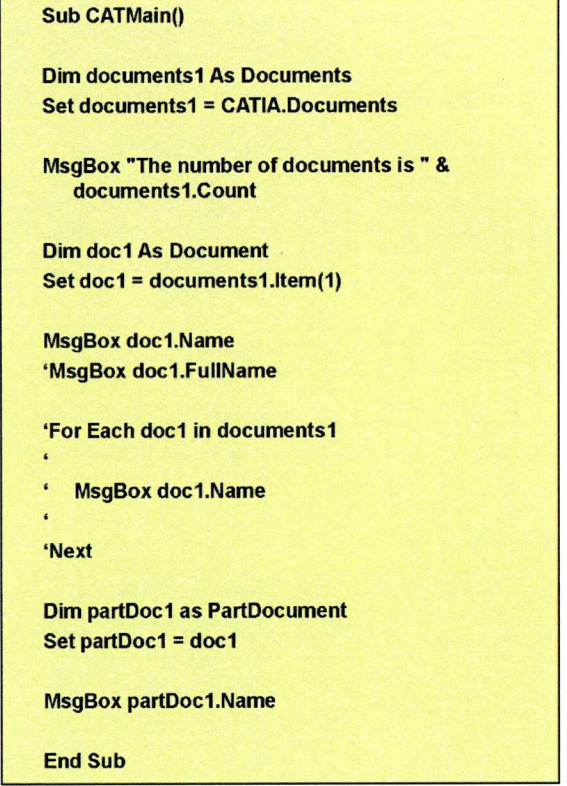

```
Sub CATMain()

Dim documents1 As Documents
Set documents1 = CATIA.Documents

MsgBox "The number of documents is " &
    documents1.Count

Dim doc1 As Document
Set doc1 = documents1.Item(1)

MsgBox doc1.Name
'MsgBox doc1.FullName

'For Each doc1 in documents1
'
'    MsgBox doc1.Name
'
'Next

Dim partDoc1 as PartDocument
Set partDoc1 = doc1

MsgBox partDoc1.Name

End Sub
```

Step 7

Note that the PartDocument object "partDoc1" is "Set" to the Document object "doc1". The setting of a variable to an object of a different type is possible in this case because the PartDocument class "inherits" from the Document class. This is depicted in the CATIA object diagram below. Not only does PartDocument inherit from Document, but so does ProductDocument, DrawingDocument, etc.

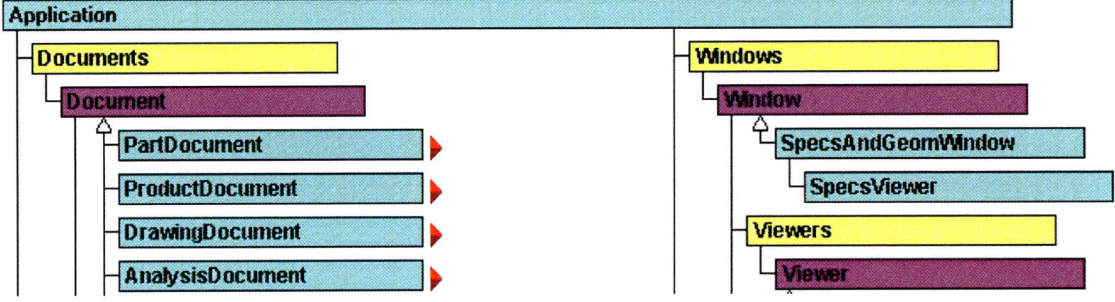

Step 8

- Modify the previous code as shown in the code window to the right by adding the line:
  partDoc1.Close

- Note in the Intellisense drop-down that the "Close" method has a green icon to indicate that it is a method as apposed to a property.

- The icon for a property can be seen for the property "FullName"

- Run the new code using the "Run" button

- Note that the calling of this "Close" method performs the action of closing the document

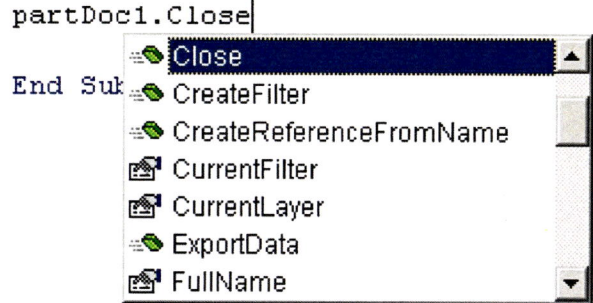

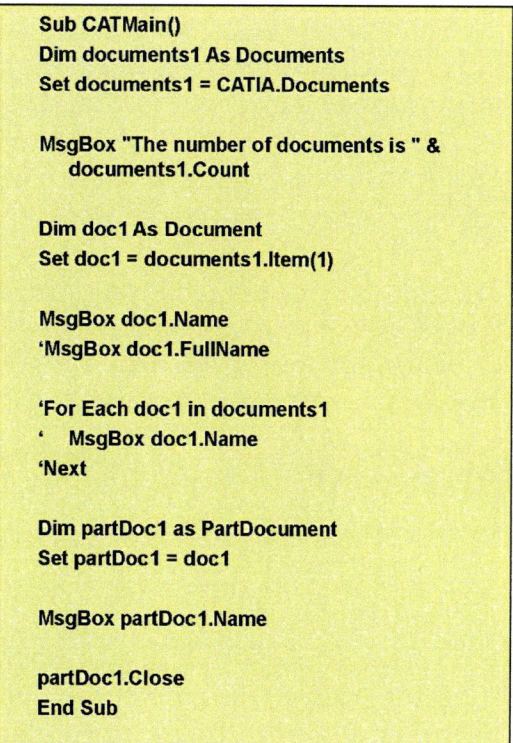

```
Sub CATMain()
Dim documents1 As Documents
Set documents1 = CATIA.Documents

MsgBox "The number of documents is " &
    documents1.Count

Dim doc1 As Document
Set doc1 = documents1.Item(1)

MsgBox doc1.Name
'MsgBox doc1.FullName

'For Each doc1 in documents1
'    MsgBox doc1.Name
'Next

Dim partDoc1 as PartDocument
Set partDoc1 = doc1

MsgBox partDoc1.Name

partDoc1.Close
End Sub
```

Workshop 4 – Conclusion

This concludes Workshop 4. In this workshop you have learned to:

- Access the properties of objects

- Iterate through the items of a collection

- Set a variable of one type to an object of another type that it inherits from

- Call the methods of objects

Chapter 4: Error Handling

When writing CATIA macros (or any macros), it's a good idea to avoid any errors at all cost. Don't let your users think, they are "only users". Write them out of the equation. It is important to debug your programs to avoid errors and program crashes. Trust me, it's not much fun if another user runs a code and tells the programmer "Hey, your code doesn't work." Thus, the goal is to never have a code break because of a run-time error. If you can't avoid an error then use some form of error handling.

Even if the program you write has the correct syntax, it may still encounter a "run time" error as it is running. This is why error handling is necessary. For example, the following code would produce an error if the "ActiveDocument" in CATIA was a CATProduct and not a part.

```
Sub CATMain()
    Dim pdoc1 as PartDocument
    Set pdoc1 = CATIA.ActiveDocument
    MsgBox pdoc1.FullName

End Sub
```

The program would stop at the third line of the above code. By using the statement "On Error Resume Next", the program will ignore errors that are generated and proceed through the subsequent lines. However, in this example where an error is ignored and the program proceeds, another error is generated on the next line. This is because the variable "pdoc1" is "Nothing." It wasn't successfully "Set" in the previous line.

```
On Error Resume Next
Dim pdoc1 as PartDocument
Set pdoc1 = CATIA.ActiveDocument
MsgBox pdoc1.FullName
```

The behavior of the program can be made even more intelligent by using the "Err" object, which is an object that exists in every VBA program. The Err object holds information regarding errors that have been generated. The "number" property of the "Err" object indicates whether an error has been generated or not.

```
Sub CATMain()
On Error Resume Next
    Dim pdoc1 as PartDocument
    Set pdoc1 = CATIA.ActiveDocument
    If Err.Number = 0 Then
        MsgBox pdoc1.FullName
    Else

MsgBox "Active document is not a part document!"
End If
```

```
End Sub
```

Calling the "Clear" method on the Err object sets the "Number" property of the Err object to zero ("clean the slate" as they say).

```
SubCATMain()
On Error Resume Next
'Insert  various  programming  statements  here  along  with  logic  and_
conditionals that deal with errors that are generated. Assume Err.number_
 is not zero after these statements run

Err.Clear
     'Proceed with the error number cleared (Err.number is now zero)
End Sub
```

The command "On Error Goto 0" sets the execution of the program so that errors aren't ignored for the subsequent lines.

```
Sub CATMain()

On Error Resume Next
' If a runtime error occurs here, the program proceeds
On Error Goto 0
' Now when a runtime error occurs, the program will stop
End Sub
```

You want to write your code to avoid any interruptions due to errors at all costs.

```
'turns off the built-in program interruption error
On Error Resume Next

'this command might or might not fail depending on whether the Part is in_
session
Set oPartDoc = CATIA.Documents.Item("WASHER.CATPart")
'check whether the preceding command has failed or not (Err is built in)
```

```
If Err.Number <> 0 Then

'error handling code
MsgBox "Washer is not in session"
End
End If
'command resumes built-in program interruption on error

On Error GoTo 0
```

You can find a complete list of trappable error codes you may encounter when you use the Err function (as well as other error handling tips) here:

http://support.microsoft.com/kb/146864

Workshop 5: Navigating a Part Document with Error Handling

Learn how to effectively navigate a part with error handling and count the number of sketch based features in Workshop 5.

WORKSHOP 5

Navigating a Part Document
with Error Handling

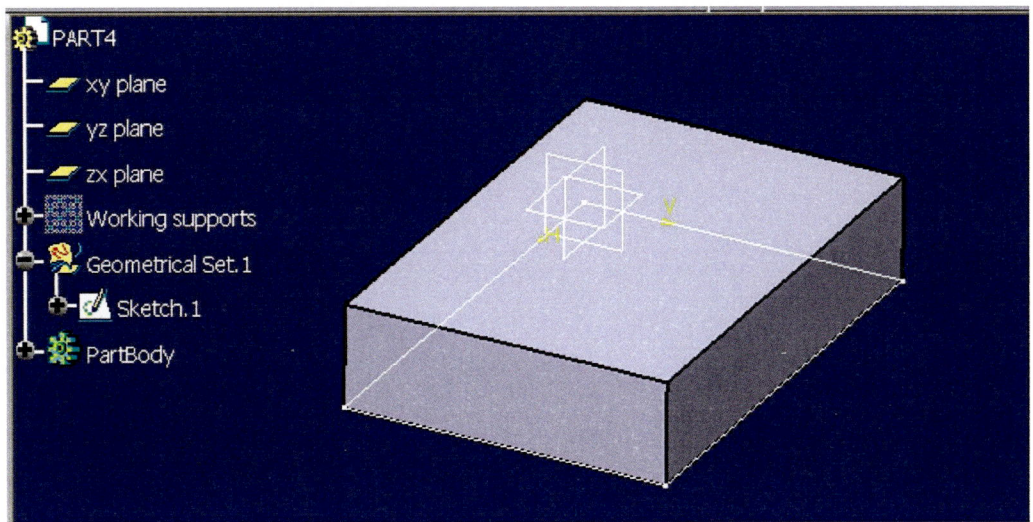

Workshop 5 – Introduction

■ Description

In this workshop you will learn to "drill down" the object structure of a part document while using error handling to deal with certain programmatic challenges.

■ Outline

1. Create a new CATPart in CATIA and create a new CATIA VBA library and module.
2. Use error handling in your code to check that the active document is a part document.
3. Have the program count the number of sketch based features and datum planes in the part using error handling.

Step 1

- First, we are going to create some geometry to test our macro on. Units and names do not matter for this exercise.
- Create a new part
- In the part design workbench, draw a sketch of a square on any plane
- Pad the sketch (to any length)
- Under Geometrical Set 1, create an offset plane and a datum (explicit) plane

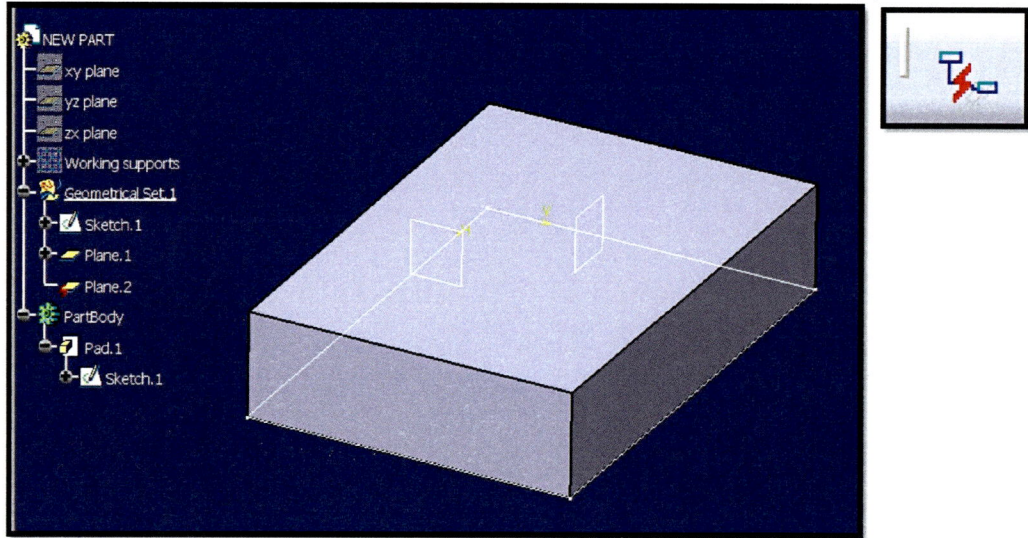

Step 2

- Create a new module in the myVBA macro library called NavigatePart
- Enter the code shown below
- With the new part open, run the code using either the play button or the Tools > Macro > Macros menu.
  NOTE: Nothing happens
- Now, create a new product document and leave it open in CATIA as the active document. Run the code again and the message box should appear

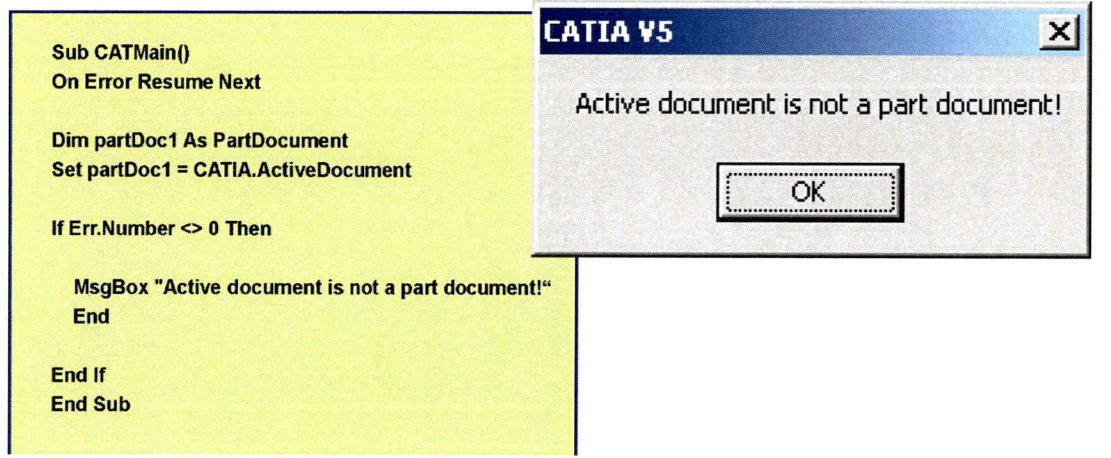

```vb
Sub CATMain()
On Error Resume Next

Dim partDoc1 As PartDocument
Set partDoc1 = CATIA.ActiveDocument

If Err.Number <> 0 Then

    MsgBox "Active document is not a part document!"
    End

End If
End Sub
```

Step 3

Open the V5Automation.chm file and go to the object diagram for part documents. The first goal is to add code that will count the number of sketch-based-features. These feature objects are all different kinds of "shapes". The diagram shows that we will have to "drill down" like so: Part > Bodies > Body > Shapes. Click on the red arrow next to the "Shape" box to see a more detailed view of Shape objects.

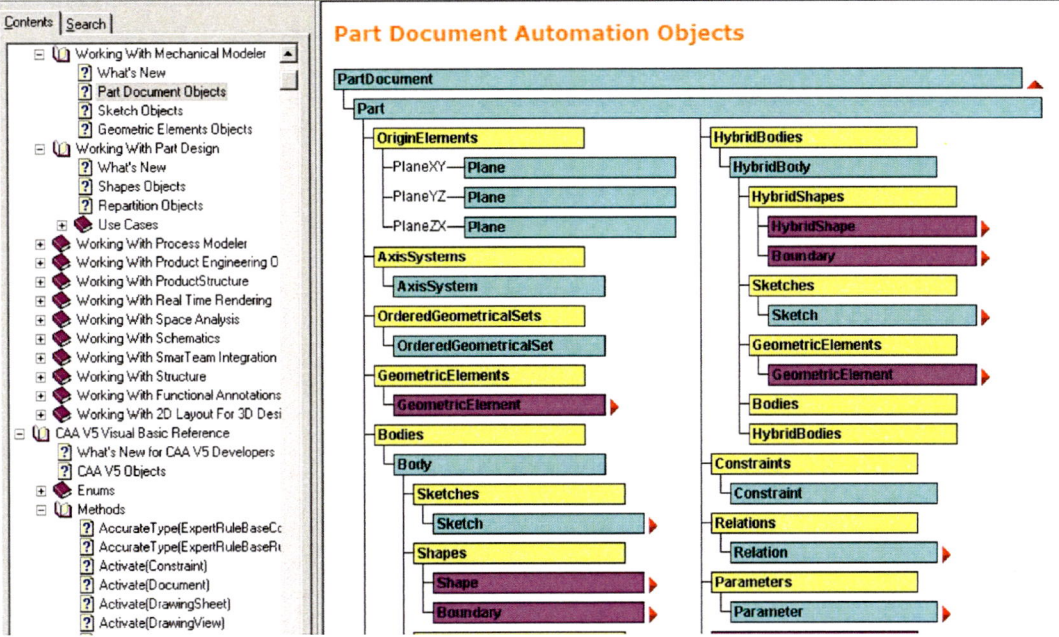

Step 4: Use the Shape Object Diagram

As you can see, there are many classes that inherit from the more general Shape class. Here you can see SketchBasedShape, BooleanShape, DressUpShape, and TransformationShape. We want to count the number of SketchBasedShape objects that are in the part.

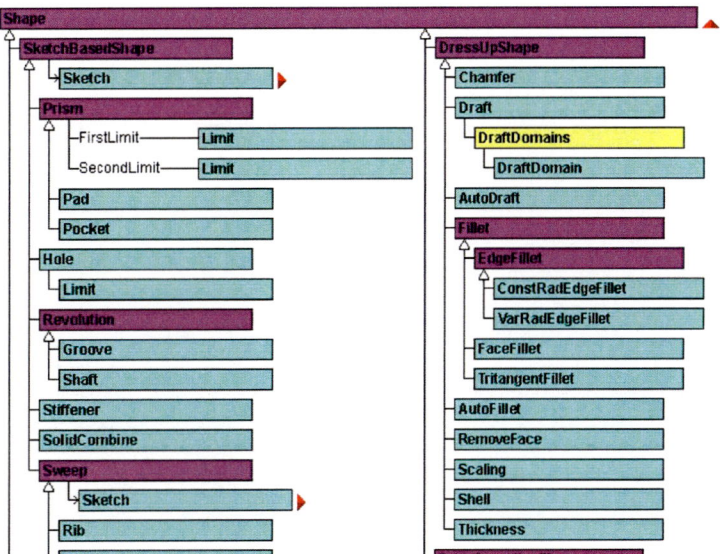

Step 4: Add Code to Count SketchBasedShape Objects

- Add the code shown to the right to the previously entered code. Note that this first section of code "grabs" the Shapes collection underneath the first part body.

- This next section of code prepares the variables we will use to "grab" individual objects from the Shapes collection

- The for each loop "grabs" each Shape in the Shapes collection, then attempts to set the more specific SketchBasedShape object to the more abstract Shape object. If the Shape object is in fact a SketchBasedShape, then no error is generated. If no error is generated, then the "sketchShapeCount" is increased by 1.

- Note that the Error object "Err" must be cleared each time so that errors don"t "carry over" to the next iteration of the loop. Run the code, you should see this message box:

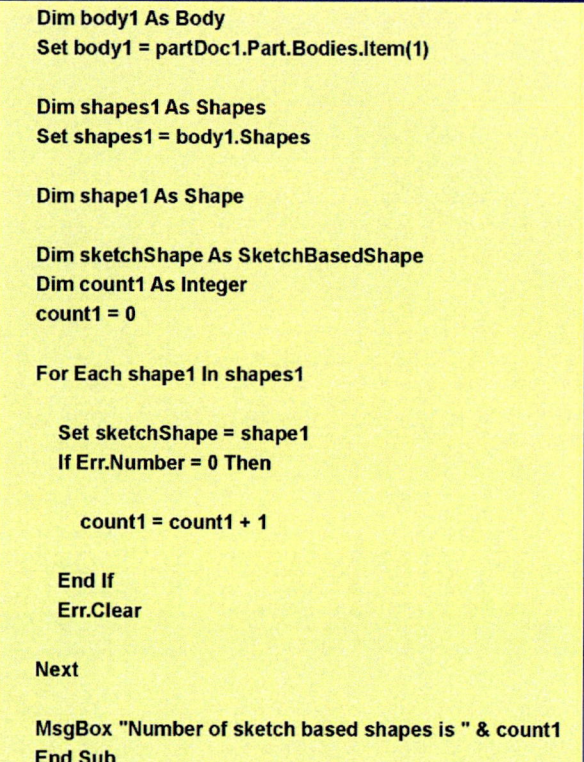

```
CATIA V5                              [X]

Number of sketch based shapes is 1

        [    OK    ]
```

```
Dim body1 As Body
Set body1 = partDoc1.Part.Bodies.Item(1)

Dim shapes1 As Shapes
Set shapes1 = body1.Shapes

Dim shape1 As Shape

Dim sketchShape As SketchBasedShape
Dim count1 As Integer
count1 = 0

For Each shape1 In shapes1

    Set sketchShape = shape1
    If Err.Number = 0 Then

        count1 = count1 + 1

    End If
    Err.Clear

Next

MsgBox "Number of sketch based shapes is " & count1
End Sub
```

Step 5: Add Code to Count BooleanShape Objects

Another method for counting the number of sketch based features is the For Next loop.

Note the Item(1) in the code. This means we will only look at the first geometrical set within a part file. If you want to expand the code you could add another loop to go through all geometrical sets within a catpart.

```
Dim body1 As Body
Set body1 = partDoc1.Part.Bodies.Item(1)

Dim shapes1 As Shapes
Set shapes1 = body1.Shapes

shapecount = shapes1.count

Dim shape1 As Shape

Dim sketchShape As SketchBasedShape
Dim count1 As Integer
count1 = 0

For i = 1 To shapecount

    Set sketchShape = shapes1.Item(i)
    If Err.Number = 0 Then

        count1 = count1 + 1

    End If

    Err.Clear
```

Step 6: Use the Part Document Object Diagram

Return to the part document object diagram of the .chm documentation (picture on the following page). Note that the Part object has a collection called HybridBodies. This is a collection of all the geometrical sets of the part, but the programmatic name of a geometrical set is HybridBody. We want to add code to count the number of datum planes. A datum plane is a hybrid shape, but we don"t know for sure what it"s programmatic name is. Click on the red arrow indicated below to go to the object diagram for the HybridShape object.

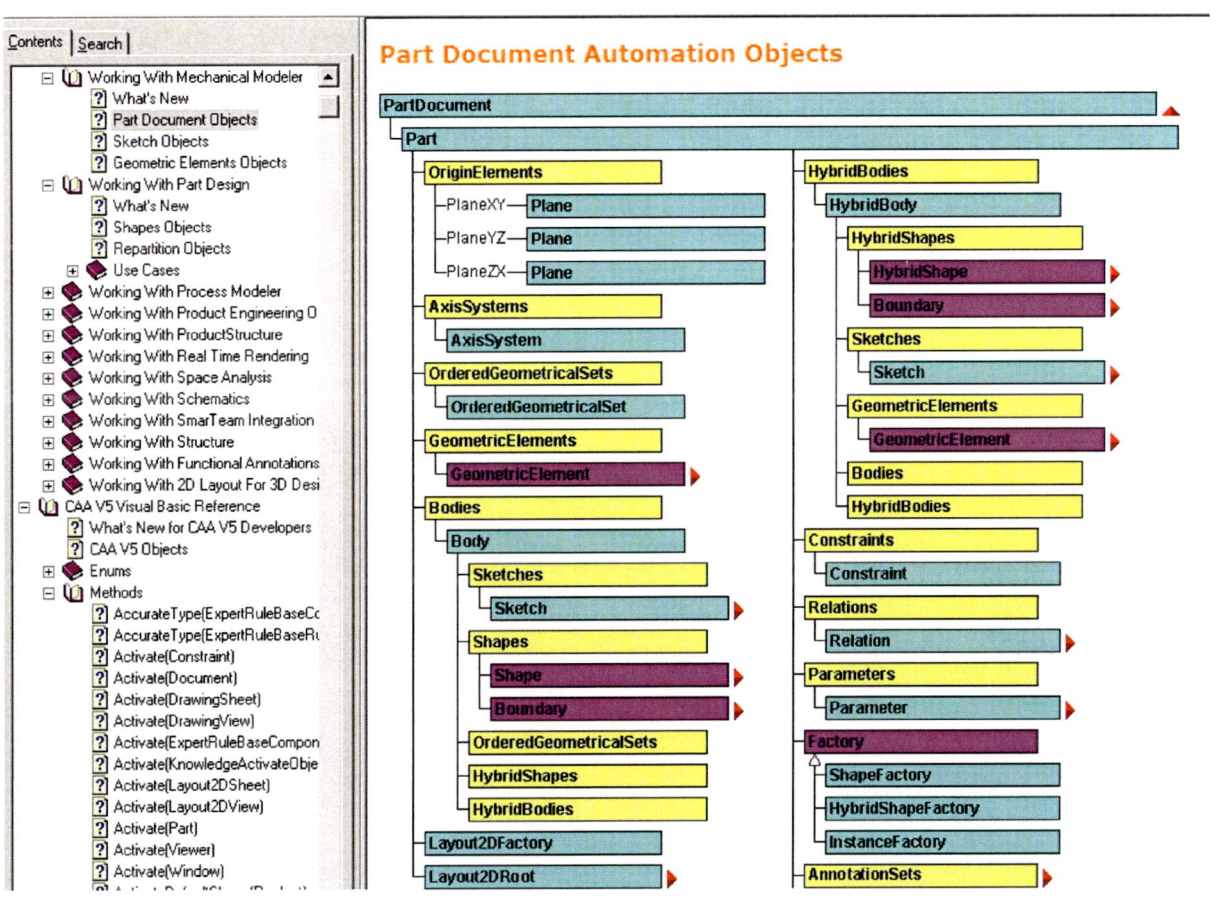

Step 7: Use the HybridShape Object Diagram

There are many classes that inherit from the abstract class HybridShape, as can be seen below. We are looking for a class that is the equivalent of a datum plane. The class HybridShapePlaneExplicit looks like the right one.

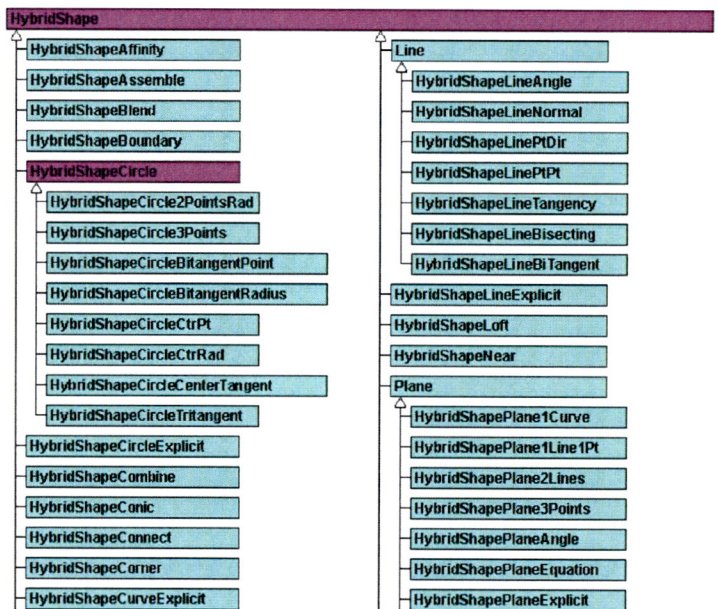

Step 8: Add Code to Count Datum Planes

Insert the following code below what we already have. You should get the resulting message box.

```
Set part1 = partDoc1.Part

Dim hybridShapeFactory1 As HybridShapeFactory
Set hybridShapeFactory1 = part1.HybridShapeFactory

Dim hybridBodies1 As HybridBodies
Set hybridBodies1 = part1.HybridBodies

Dim hybridBody1 As HybridBody
Set hybridBody1 = hybridBodies1.Item(1)
geocount = hybridBody1.HybridShapes.count

Dim k, count2 As Integer
Dim datumPlane As HybridShapePlaneExplicit
count2 = 0
```

```
For k = 1 To geocount

Set datumPlane = hybridBody1.HybridShapes.Item(k)
    If Err.Number = 0 Then

        count2 = count2 + 1

    End If
    Err.Clear

Next
MsgBox "Number of sketch based shapes is: " &
count1 & vbNewLine & _
        "Number of datum planes is : " & count2

End Sub
```

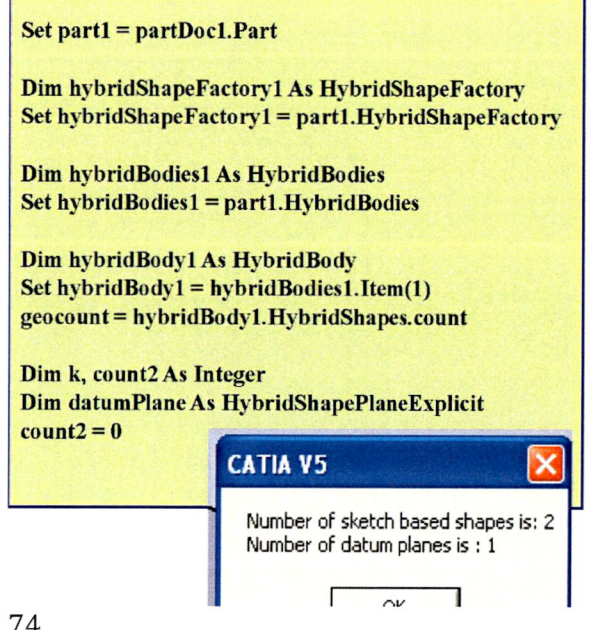

Workshop 5 – Conclusion

This concludes Workshop 5. In this workshop you have learned to:

•Use the object diagrams found in the ".chm" file to understand CATIA objects

•Navigate the structure of a CATIA part document by iterating through the various collections that a part contains

•Access the Shapes collection under a part Body object in order to iterate through features of the part

•Access the HybridShapes collection under a HybridBody (Geometrical Set) to iterate through various 3D geometry

Chapter 5: Geometry Creation

Factories are objects that do not have a corresponding object in interactive CATIA but are required to create any type of geometry. Units passed on to a Factory must be in millimeters. Factories differ depending on the type of geometry being created:

- **Factory2D**: used to created 2D sketches
- **ShapeFactory**: used to create solid geometry
- **HybridShapeFactory**: used to create wireframe and surface geometry

Sketching in Part Design

A "sketch" is an object that contains a collection of 2D geometry and constraints which are created on a plane. To create new sketches use the Add method of the Sketches collection. This creates a brand new sketch and adds it to the tree but does not actually start the sketcher. The **OpenEdition** method must be started to begin sketching. Every time you begin a sketch you must also close out of the sketch (just like you open and close sketcher when doing it by hand). To create a new sketch on the XY plane:

```
Dim oSketch As Sketch
Set oSketch=oBody.Sketches.Add("XY")
Dim oF As Factory2D
Set oF = oSketch.OpenEdition()
'insert 2d geometry creation here
oSketch.CloseEdition()
```

To add a new point in the sketch at coordinates x=10mm and y=45mm:

```
Dim oPt As Point2D
Set oPt=oF.CreatePoint(10,45)
```

Sketches are recordable. Pay attention to your settings while recording macros as CATIA could automatically create constraints as you draw the sketch geometry. To create a line:

```
Dim line2D1 As Line2D
Set line2D1 = oF.CreateLine(0,0,10,45)
```

In order to have our newly created line actually connect with our first point we need to define the end point of the line like so:

```
Line2D1.EndPoint = oPt
```

To sketch a circle, first create a point at x=25, y=25 then define the center of the circle as the newly created point.

```
Dim oCircPt As Point2D
Set oCircPt = oF.CreatePoint(25, 25)
Dim circle2D1 As Circle2D
Set circle2D1 = oF.CreateClosedCircle(45,38,36) 'enter any points for now
Circle2D1.CenterPoint = oCircPt
```

Again, record a macro while sketching (and remember to exit the sketcher before stopping the recorder) to see what information is needed.

Solid Objects

ShapeFactory is used to create solid objects such as pads, pockets, holes, etc. To create a new 40mm pad using the sketch named "SketchRect" get the ShapeFactory for the part then create the pad:

```
Dim oSF As ShapeFactory
Set oSF = oPartDoc.Part.ShapeFactory
Dim oPad1 As Pad
Set oPad1 =oSF.CreatePad(SketchRect,40)
Part1.Update
```

You must update the part manually when creating objects with macros. You have to update the part before adding dress-up features like chamfers and fillets. Order also matters when recording macros for sketch based features.

References and Sketch Constraints

For certain functions within the CATIA object model it is required pass the function through a reference object instead of to the object directly. To create references:

```
Dim oRef As Reference
Set oRef = oPart.CreateReferenceFromObject(oPlane)
```

References can be used when creating constraints for our newly created lines we created in sketcher.

```
Dim constraints1 As Constraints
```

```
Set constraints1 = sketch1.Constraints
Dim reference2 As Reference
Dim reference3 As Reference

Set reference2 = part1.CreateReferenceFromObject(line2D2)
Set reference3 = part1.CreateReferenceFromObject(line2D1)

Set constraint1 = constraints1.AddBiEltCst(catCstTypeHorizontality,_
reference2, reference3)
'set if constraint value drives dimension or is driven by it
constraint1.Mode = catCstModeDrivingDimension
```

To set a radius constraint for our circle sketch:

```
Dim constraints1 As Constraints
Set constraints1 = sketch1.Constraints

Dim reference4 As Reference
Set reference4 = part1.CreateReferenceFromObject(circle2D1)

Dim constraint1 As Constraint
Set constraint1 = constraints1.AddMonoEltCst(catCstTypeRadius,_
reference4)

Constraint1.Mode = catCstModeDrivingDimension
```

Wireframe Geometry

All solid features are generically called Shapes while all wireframe geometry are called HybridShapes. In the case of a Pad feature, there is only one Pad object regardless of how the pad is made. Points, however, have many different object types based on HOW the point is created, such as HybridShapePointCoord, HybridShapePointOnCurves, etc.

When switching between wireframe and solid feature creation you do NOT need to programmatically change workbenches. You DO however need to have a HybridBody set as the InWorkObject for wireframe or a Body set as the InWorkObject for solids.

```
oPart.InWorkObject = oBody1
oPart.InWorkObject = oHybridBody1
```

Datum Elements

To create object with no history or parents:

```
AddNewPointDatum()
AddNewCurveDatum()
AddNewSurfaceDatum()
```

Other objects include HybridShapePointExplicit, HybridShapeCurveExplicit, etc. Remember, all wireframe elements must be appended to the tree before they appear in interactive CATIA.

Workshop 6: Creating Sketch Geometry

Learn more about macro recording and sketching in Workshop 6.

WORKSHOP 6

Creating Sketch Geometry

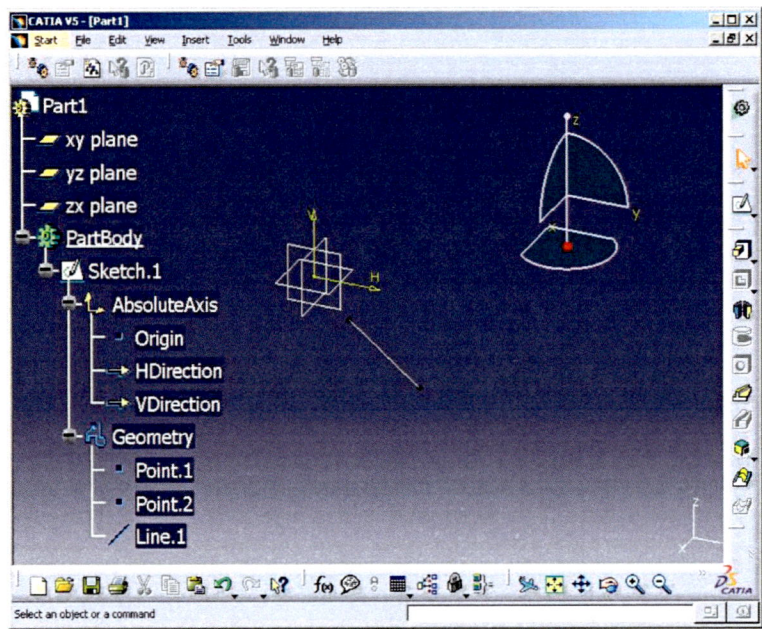

Workshop 6 – Creating Sketch Geometry

■ Description

In this workshop you will explore the creation of sketch geometry in a part document. The purpose of this is to illustrate the use of "factories" to create objects in a part document.

■ Outline

1. Start a new macro recording.

2. Create a sketch on the Y-Z plane that consists of a single line.

3. Open the recorded macro and observe what has been recorded.

4. Modify the macro to create additional geometry and rerun it on a new part document.

Step 1: Start Recording a Macro

- Create a new part document
- Start recording a new macro.
- Name it "Create_Sketch_01"

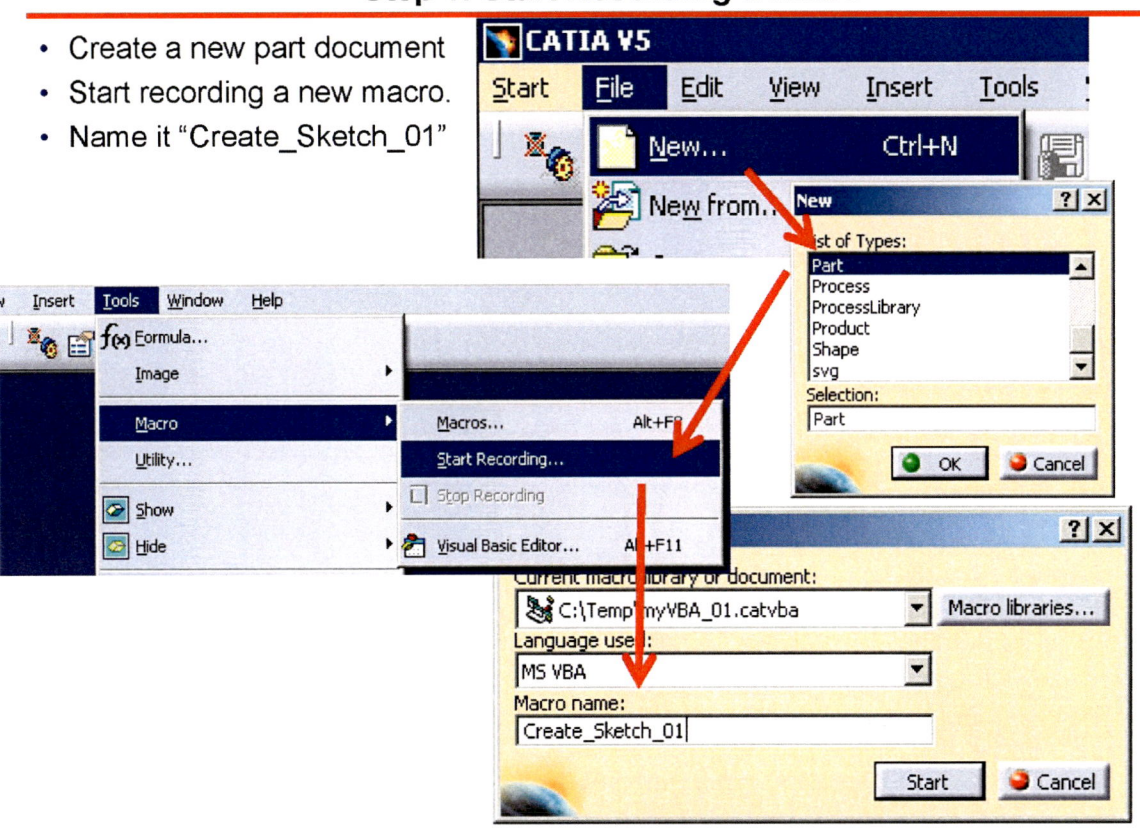

Step 2. Start the sketch

- Start a sketch with the "Sketch" button

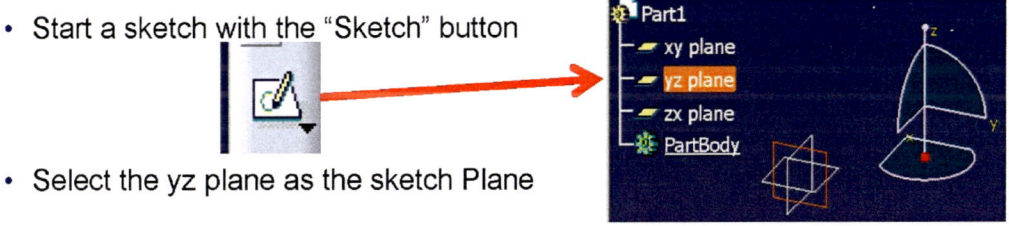

- Select the yz plane as the sketch Plane

- Create a line away from the origin that isn"t parallel to to the "V" axis or "H" axis

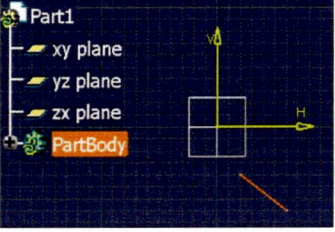

- Complete the sketch with the "Exit Workbench" button

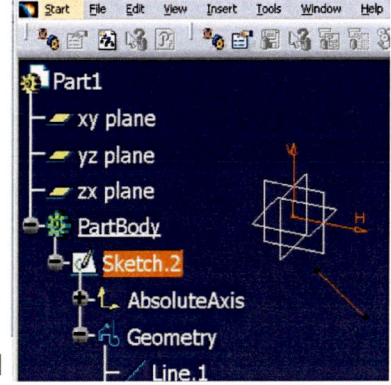

- The resulting should similar to what is pictured

Step 3: Start Commenting the Code

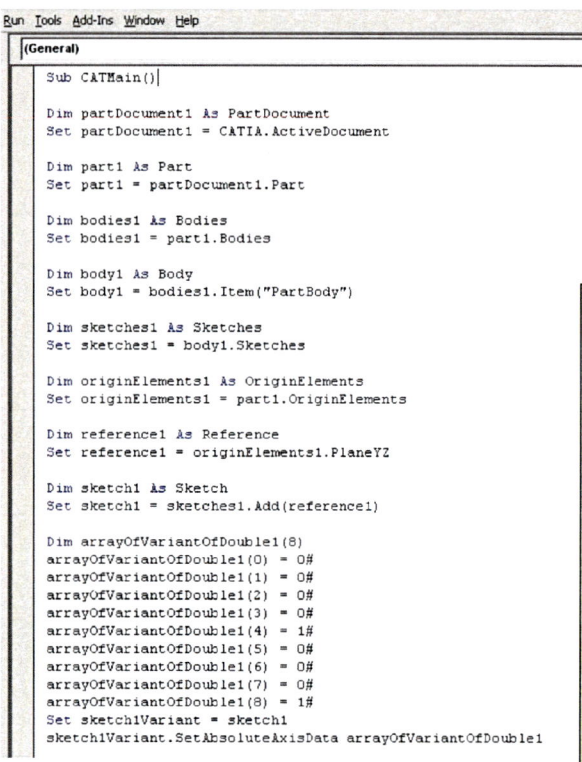

Open the CATIA VBA editor to view the code that was recorded (see left). A good first step after recording a macro is to add comments to clearly call-out the sequence of "stages" of the code. To start, add the comments seen below to call-out the first step, which is the getting of the part body.

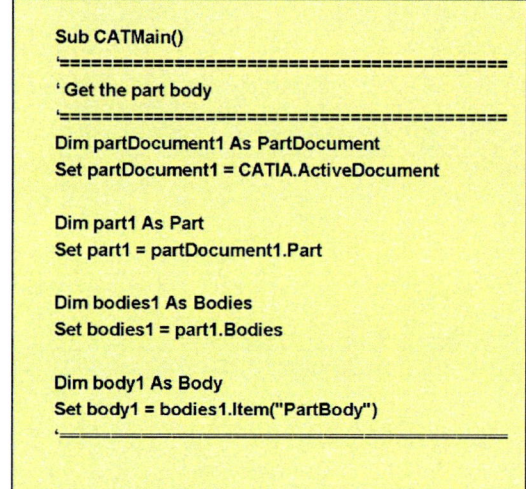

Step 4: Comment and test the code

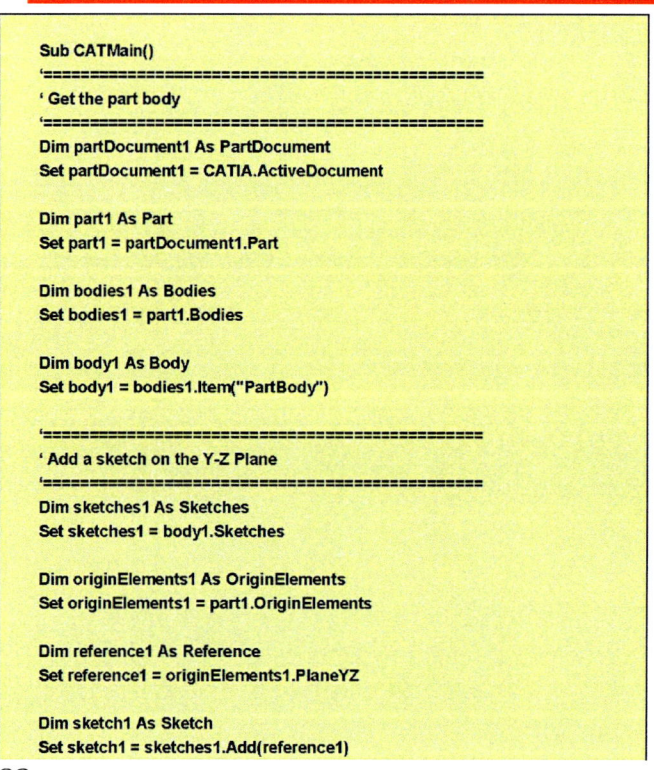

- Add these comments in order to call-out the next "stage" in the code: the addition of a sketch to the Y-Z plane

- Add this "End" command here. This will cause the macro to stop here when it is run.

- Open a new part document and run the macro. Note that the result is that a new sketch is created.

Step 5: Comment and test the code

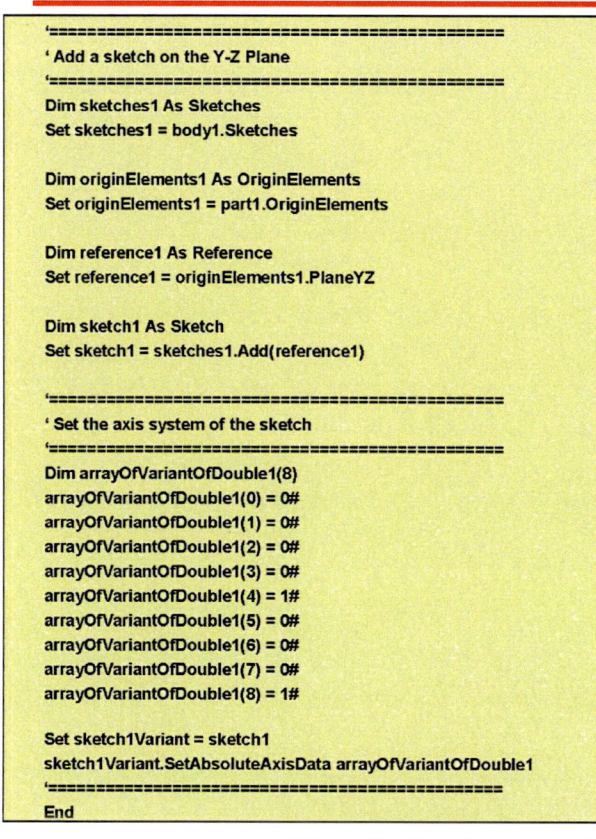

```
'===========================================
' Add a sketch on the Y-Z Plane
'===========================================
Dim sketches1 As Sketches
Set sketches1 = body1.Sketches

Dim originElements1 As OriginElements
Set originElements1 = part1.OriginElements

Dim reference1 As Reference
Set reference1 = originElements1.PlaneYZ

Dim sketch1 As Sketch
Set sketch1 = sketches1.Add(reference1)


'===========================================
' Set the axis system of the sketch
'===========================================
Dim arrayOfVariantOfDouble1(8)
arrayOfVariantOfDouble1(0) = 0#
arrayOfVariantOfDouble1(1) = 0#
arrayOfVariantOfDouble1(2) = 0#
arrayOfVariantOfDouble1(3) = 0#
arrayOfVariantOfDouble1(4) = 1#
arrayOfVariantOfDouble1(5) = 0#
arrayOfVariantOfDouble1(6) = 0#
arrayOfVariantOfDouble1(7) = 0#
arrayOfVariantOfDouble1(8) = 1#

Set sketch1Variant = sketch1
sketch1Variant.SetAbsoluteAxisData arrayOfVariantOfDouble1
'===========================================
End
```

- Remove the "End" command and add a comment to call-out the next stage:
- This next stage of code can be thought of as containing two parts:

  1. The creation of a 9 member array of variants
  2. The calling of the "SetAbsoluteAxisData" method.

  The array contains the numerical information that describes a 2D axis system that is positioned in 3D space.

  Note that a variable that isn"t dimmed (sketch1Variant) is set to the sketch object, then "SetAbsoluteAxisData" is called on it. This is a requirement: calling "SetAbsoluteAxisData" on the actual sketch object like so would cause a compile error:

  sketch1.SetAbsoluteAxisData arrayOfVariantOfDouble1

- Add the "End" command as shown.
- Open a new part document and run the macro. Note that the result is indistinguishable from the last time the macro was run. This is because the position of the axis system that is described by the array is the same as the default position.

Step 6: Replace code with simpler code

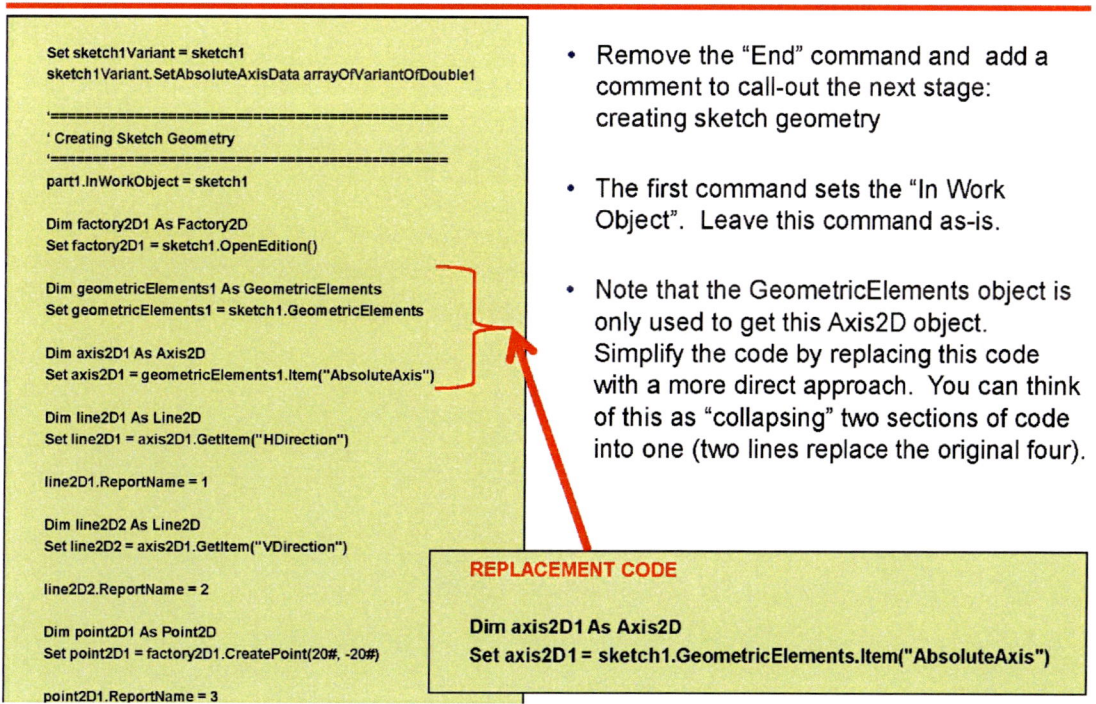

```
Set sketch1Variant = sketch1
sketch1Variant.SetAbsoluteAxisData arrayOfVariantOfDouble1


'===========================================
' Creating Sketch Geometry
'===========================================
part1.InWorkObject = sketch1

Dim factory2D1 As Factory2D
Set factory2D1 = sketch1.OpenEdition()

Dim geometricElements1 As GeometricElements
Set geometricElements1 = sketch1.GeometricElements

Dim axis2D1 As Axis2D
Set axis2D1 = geometricElements1.Item("AbsoluteAxis")

Dim line2D1 As Line2D
Set line2D1 = axis2D1.GetItem("HDirection")

line2D1.ReportName = 1

Dim line2D2 As Line2D
Set line2D2 = axis2D1.GetItem("VDirection")

line2D2.ReportName = 2

Dim point2D1 As Point2D
Set point2D1 = factory2D1.CreatePoint(20#, -20#)

point2D1.ReportName = 3
```

REPLACEMENT CODE

```
Dim axis2D1 As Axis2D
Set axis2D1 = sketch1.GeometricElements.Item("AbsoluteAxis")
```

- Remove the "End" command and add a comment to call-out the next stage: creating sketch geometry

- The first command sets the "In Work Object". Leave this command as-is.

- Note that the GeometricElements object is only used to get this Axis2D object. Simplify the code by replacing this code with a more direct approach. You can think of this as "collapsing" two sections of code into one (two lines replace the original four).

Step 7: Identify code for removal (1/3)

```
Dim line2D1 As Line2D
Set line2D1 = axis2D1.GetItem("HDirection")
line2D1.ReportName = 1

Dim line2D2 As Line2D
Set line2D2 = axis2D1.GetItem("VDirection")
line2D2.ReportName = 2

Dim point2D1 As Point2D
Set point2D1 = factory2D1.CreatePoint(20#, -20#)
point2D1.ReportName = 3

Dim point2D2 As Point2D
Set point2D2 = factory2D1.CreatePoint(60#, -50#)
point2D2.ReportName = 4

Dim line2D3 As Line2D
Set line2D3 = factory2D1.CreateLine(20#, -20#, 60#, -50#)

line2D3.ReportName = 5
line2D3.StartPoint = point2D1
line2D3.EndPoint = point2D2

sketch1.CloseEdition
part1.InWorkObject = body1
part1.Update
End Sub
```

- The commands such as "line2D1.ReportName = 1" look peculiar. They seem to serve no purpose. See the next slide for tips on how to investigate the purpose of this command.

- Note that although the recorded macro shows that a line2D1 and line2D2 were created, these objects only use is to have their "ReportName" properties set. If we determine that the setting of these values isn"t necessary, we can get rid of this section of code all together.

Step 7: Identify code for removal (2/3)

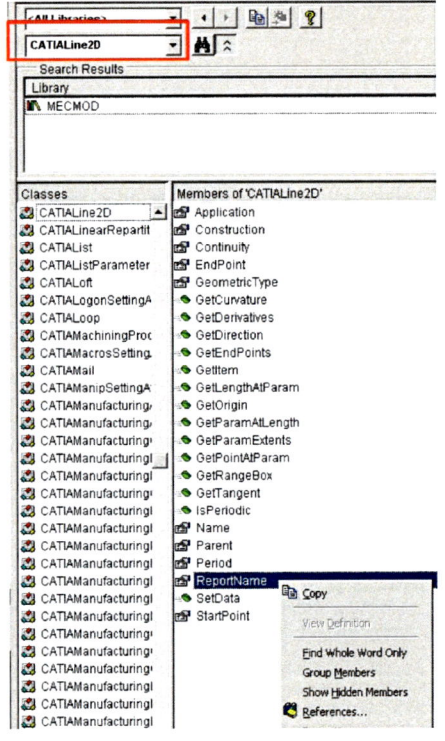

- The programming object in question is the class "Line2D". Hit F2 to enter the object browser and search "CATIALine2D"

- All the "Members" of CATIALine2D (Line2D) are listed. Right-click on "ReportName" and select "Help"

Step 7: Identify code for removal (3/3)

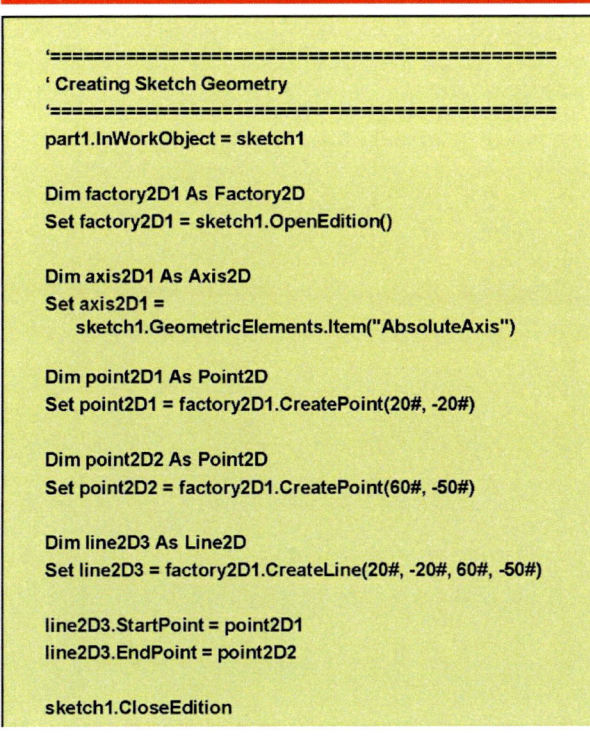

- On the documentation page that comes up, note that "Geometry2D" is the class. This is because although "ReportName" is a property of "Line2D", this property is inherited from "Geometry2D"

- The description of the ReportName property doesn't tell us much. For one, it only states that this property returns the report name, but we can see in the recorded macro that it "sets" the report name.

- For now, although the macro does use this property to "set" these report name values, assume that this is an unnecessary step, and remove these lines of code.

Step 8: Renaming and more code removal

```
'=======================================
' Creating Sketch Geometry
'=======================================
part1.InWorkObject = sketch1

Dim factory2D1 As Factory2D
Set factory2D1 = sketch1.OpenEdition()

Dim axis2D1 As Axis2D
Set axis2D1 =
    sketch1.GeometricElements.Item("AbsoluteAxis")

Dim point2D1 As Point2D
Set point2D1 = factory2D1.CreatePoint(20#, -20#)

Dim point2D2 As Point2D
Set point2D2 = factory2D1.CreatePoint(60#, -50#)

Dim line2D3 As Line2D
Set line2D3 = factory2D1.CreateLine(20#, -20#, 60#, -50#)

line2D3.StartPoint = point2D1
line2D3.EndPoint = point2D2

sketch1.CloseEdition
```

- This stage of code, after modifications, is shown to the left
- Note that first two points are created, and it appears as though the line gets created by using the same coordinates of the points.
- The "StartPoint" property and "EndPoint" property need to be explicitly set to the two points that were created.
- In order to increase the clarity of the code, many objects could be renamed in a more descriptive manner. The Point2D object "point2D1" could be named "pt2Dstart", and "point2D2" could be named "pt2Dend".

Workshop 6 – Conclusion

This concludes Workshop 6. In this workshop you have learned to:

•Start a CATIA VBA program by first recording a macro

•Record the creation of a single line in a sketch

•How to edit a recorded macro by using comments, by renaming variables, and by deleting unnecessary lines, for the purpose of increasing clarity and simplicity in the code

•How to use the object browser and help documentation to investigate unknown API properties and methods

The Selection Object

To interactively access properties of an object in CATIA V5 you would simply right click on the object and select properties. The object has to be selected first. In the CATIA object model, there is a special object called "selection" which belongs to different documents. This Selection object is a container that holds anything that is currently selected in a session of CATIA V5. It can be accessed like this:

```
Dim oSelection As Selection
Set oSelection = CATIA.ActiveDocument.Selection
```

If an element is added to the Selection in a macro, the element will highlight as selected in the CATIA window. You can add elements to the selection using the Add and Search methods. Other methods include cut, copy, paste, delete, hide, and show. After you're done performing actions with the selected objects you need to clear the selection using the Clear method. The complete process is: (1) add elements to the selection, (2) perform the desired actions with the selected elements, and finally (3) clear the selection. If nothing is selected then the selection is empty. If one or more objects are selected then the selection contains those one or more objects.

To add an element to the selection:

```
Dim oSel As Selection
Set oSel = CATIA.ActiveDocument.Selection
oSel.Clear
oSel.Add(ObjectToAdd)
```

A good practice is to always clear the selection before and after you use it. To check what has been selected you could use the following code, which will loop through all selected objects and display the name in a message box for each one:

```
For I = 1 to oSel.Count
      MsgBox oSel.Item(i).Value.Name
Next 'i
```

One of the most common uses of selecting an object in CATIA is to search through that object. Interactively in CATIA you can search for elements or element groups using the Edit + Search pull-down menu. You can do the same thing through VB using the Selection object. You can search by several different methods including "Name", "Type", "Color", etc. – all the same search options available interactively.

To look for all objects named "pad":

Method 1: `oSel.Search"Name=Pad.*,all"`
Method 2: `oSearch("Name=Weld_Center*,all")`

To look for all points: `oSel.Search "Type=Point,all"`
To look for only items in the selection colored red: `oSel.Search "Color=Red,sel"`
To look for all items on layer 10: `oSel.Search "Layer=10,all"`

The selection object can also be used for a variety of other tasks:

Copy elements: `objSel.Copy`
Pasting elements: `objSel.Paste`
Delete elements: `objSel.Delete`

If you want to select all points named "WELD_PT" under any and all geometrical sets you can select the active document as your selection and search it for a specific name:

```
Sub CATMain()
Dim objSel As Selection
Set objSel =CATIA.ActiveDocument.Selection
objSel.Search("Name=WELD_PT*,all")
objcount = objSel.count
msgbox objcount
End Sub
```

Once the search command has been issued, you can then loop through the selection object to get the items that have been found using a For...Next Loop. For example, to incrementally add a number to the end of the point name:

```
Dim i As Integer
For i = 1 to objSel.Count
objSel.Item(i).Value.Name = objSel.Item(i).Value.Name&i
Next 'i
```

The process for copying and pasting an element into another element is:

1. Put the source object into the selection
2. Call cut or copy
3. Put the destination object into the selection
4. Call Paste or PasteSpecial

Exercise 5.1 Delete a Geometrical Set

In this exercise you are going to use Selection to delete a geometrical set. First, create a new CATPart with a geometrical set. Now complete the recommended macro steps:

1. Declare the selection
2. Declare the geometrical set
3. Add the geometrical set to the selection
4. Delete the geometrical set

See the back of the book for one possible solution.

Graphic Properties

The word "Get" means to obtain or retrieve information while the term "Set" means to change the information (i.e. SetRealWidth). The **VisPropertySet** object contains many methods useful for changing graphic properties such as hide/show, retrieve or set the color, opacity, line type, thickness, symbol type for points, and more.

```
Dim VisProps As VisPropertySet
Set VisProps = oSel.VisProperties
'gets the color
    VisProps.GetRealColor(255,0,0)
'sets the color
    visProps.SetRealColor(255,0,0,1)
    VisProps.SetShow(...) 'set show or hide
```

Use the selection object to hide all planes:

```
Dim oSel As Selection
Set oSel = CATIA.ActiveDocument.Selection
oSel.Search "type:Plane,all"
oSel.VisProperties.SetShow catVisPropertyNoShowAttr
oSel.Clear
```

Changing the Background

Background Color can be set by passing values to or from an array. One use of changing the background color may be to take a screen capture with a white background for easy printing (and using less ink)! Use this code to change the background color to white:

```
'This array holds the original
'ReDim is a vb function used to resize arrays
ReDim dblBackArray(2)
'background color
objViewer3D.GetBackgroundColor(dblBackArray)
'This array will hold the white color
ReDim dblWhiteArray(2)
'(the 3 values of this array are the standard RGB values but instead of_
0-255 the values are normalized)

dblWhiteArray(0) = 1
dblWhiteArray(1) = 1
dblWhiteArray(2) = 1
objViewer3D.SetBackgroundColor(dblWhiteArray)

'To change the color back:
objViewer3D.SetBackgroundColor(dblBackArray)
```

Exercise 5.2 Paste Special

In this exercise, you are going to use paste special. First, open a new part. Create a new plane inside the default geometrical set (probably called GeometricalSet.1) offset from the xy plane 50mm. Now, write a macro to copy and paste that geometrical as special into a newly created part. When you run the macro it should create a new part with the copied geometrical set and within that should be the dead plane with no history. The steps are:

1. Set the first part as the active document
2. Set a selection
3. Define the geometrical set
4. Copy the geometrical set

5. Create a new part
6. Rename the new part "Weld Station"
7. Set the destination to copy the geometrical set
8. Use CATPrtResultWithOutLink to paste special and break the links

Chapter 6: User Interaction

Besides the message and input boxes discussed earlier, there are multiple ways for users to interact with CATIA either before or during a macro program, either through selections or forms.

Interactive User Selections

Not to be confused with the selection object, **interactive selection** is when a CATIA user physically selects an element in interactive CATIA, either from the specification tree or in the graphical area. There are two main types of interactive selections: before the macro is run or while the macro is running.

Pre-Selection

Pre-selection requires a user to select elements in CATIA before the macro is initiated. When the macro is ran the elements are already in the selection object. The Item method can then be used to retrieve the element from the Selection collection. To get the first selected element:

```
Dim oSel As SelectedElement
Set oSel = oSel.Item(1)
```

The FindObject method can be used to find elements within the selection based on their type. For example, to find a 3D point:

```
Dim oPnt As Point
Set oPnt = oSel.FindObject("CATIAHybridShapePoint")
```

Selection While Running

There are three different methods to allow a user to make a selection while the macro is running and each is found under the Selection object.

- **SelectElement2:** only 1 item will be selected
- **SelectElement3:** multiple selections are required
- **SelectElement4:** single or multiple selections from non-active documents

The first requirement is a string array containing the element types you want the end user to be allowed to select. For example, if you want the user to select a point created by coordinates:

```
ReDim strArray(0)
strArray(0)="HybridShapePointCoord"
```

To allow the user more options simply change the size of the array (remember arrays start at 0 while items start at 1). The size of the array must also match exactly the number of elements in the array. In this example, the user can select the two types of points specified but nothing else:

```
ReDim strArray(1)
strArray(0)="HybridShapePointCoord"
strArray(1)="HybridShapePointOnCurve"
```

If you would rather the user is allowed to select any and all points use this:

```
ReDim strArray(0)
strArray(0)="Point"
```

Take notice that these are points only and not vertices. The order of elements in the array is also important. If you entered Line and Point into an array in that order then the line must be selected first and then the point. To help guide the user as to what needs to be selected you can display text in the bottom left hand corner of the screen to direct them what to do.

```
strText = "Please select a Line first then a Point, or select UNDO to
cancel."
```

Exercise: Write a macro asking the user to select a point:

```
'create the object array
ReDim strArray(0)
strArray(0)="Point"

'create a message
Dim msg1 As String
Msg1="Select a point or select UNDO to cancel."

'run the selection code
Dim myPoint As String
myPoint=oSelection.SelectElement2(strArray, msg1, False)
If(msg1="UNDO") Or (msg1 = "Cancel") Then
      MsgBox "You have chosen to Undo this operation."
      Exit Sub
End If
'set the object that the user selected
Set myObject = oSelection.Item(1).Value
```

SelectElement3 Example:

The following example will show you several useful CATIA programming basics, including:

1. Prompt the user to select multiple parts
2. Search selected parts for a specific element
3. Copy and paste the element into a new part

As usual, I have inserted my comments in the code to help you follow along.

```
'Every CATScript begins with this statement
Sub CATMain()
'start by declaring the selection
Dim oSel As Selection
Set oSel = CATIA.ActiveDocument.Selection
'Create an array for CATParts
ReDim strArray(0)
strArray(0)="Part"
'Display a messagebox prompting the user to select CATIA parts
Dim sStatus As String
Msgbox "Please select parts to weld."
'SelectElement3 is used to allow user to select multiple parts from the spec
tree or the Interactive area
sStatus = oSel.SelectElement3(strArray, "Select parts", False,
CATMultiSelTriggWhenUserValidatesSelection, false)
'CATMultiSelTriggWhenUserValidatesSelection option displays the following
handy little toolbar:
```

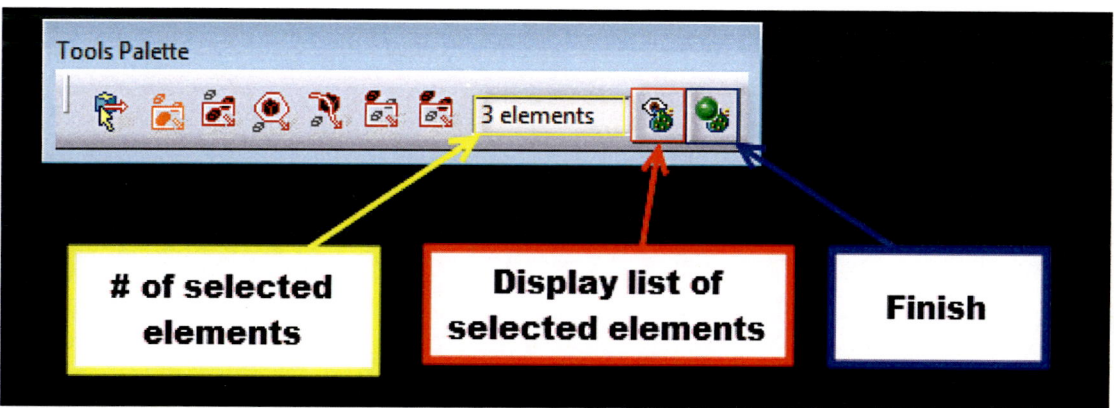

```
'Count the number of selected parts
iCount = oSel.Count

'Create a For...Next loop to cycle through all selected parts
'Isn't vb scripting fun?
For i= 1 to iCount
```

```
Dim myObject2
Set myObject2 = oSel.Item(i).value
'Search only the selected objects for the object named "PartBody"
oSel.Search "Name=PartBody,sel"

'now we take all the PartBody objects found and copy them
ReDim copies(iCount)
For k=1 to iCount
Set copies(k)=oSel.Item(k).Value
oSel.Add copies(k)
oSel.Copy
'close the loops
Next 'k
Next 'i
'Now use CATIA scripting basics to create a new part
Dim part2
Set part2 = CATIA.Documents.Add("CATPart")
Dim partDocument2 As PartDocument
'rename the new part
part2.Product.PartNumber = "My New Part"
'optional step: create a new geometrical set and rename it
Dim GSet1 As HybridBody
Set GSet1 = part2.Part.HybridBodies.Item(1)
GSet1.Name = "My Geometry"
'set the newly create part to the active document
Set partDocument2= CATIA.ActiveDocument
Dim ActSel As Selection
Set ActSel=partDocument2.Selection
ActSel.Add GSet1
'paste special the PartBody objects from the original file and paste 'as
result without link
ActSel.PasteSpecial("CATPrtResultWithOutLink" )
'clear the selection
ActSel.Clear
End Sub
```

Exercise 6.1 Delete Deactivated Features

This next exercise is a CATScript to help you clean up your CATIA files before submitting them to your boss or customers to by automatically deleting all deactivated features. The code has two main steps:

1. Displays the number of deactivated features within a part document
2. Gives the user the option to delete all the deactivated components (minus sketches)

This is accomplished by using a process called "selection and search." A CATPart is the active document which is declared as the selection. Next, search the selection for all deactivated components, meaning features whose activity status is set to false:

94

```
selection1.Search "CATPrtSearch.PartDesign Feature.Activity=FALSE"
```

Finally, use the Count function to display the number of deactivated features the code found and finally ask the user if they want to delete all the deactivated components using a *vbyesno* message box. Pictured below is a flowchart and the solution can be found in the back of the book.

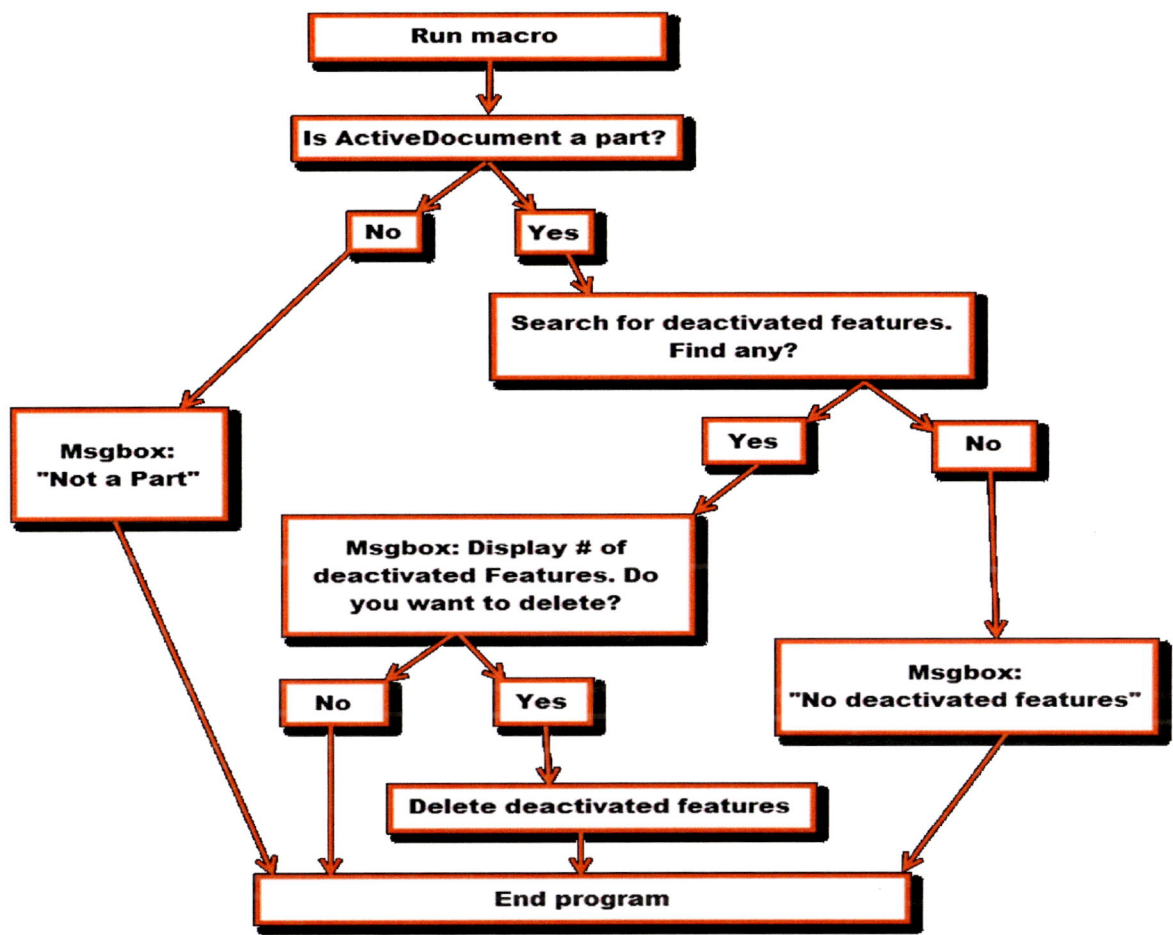

User Forms

A great way to enhance the experience for your end users and one of the most important features of Visual Basic programs is by creating userforms. Userforms give you the ability to quickly and easily create graphical user interfaces (GUI) for your macro programs. The foundation of any GUI in a Visual Basic program is a "Form" onto which various buttons, text fields, list fields, etc. may be dragged onto. Users can input text, choose from a list of options, our click a command button which runs a subroutine that uses the user input options.

Forms, buttons, text fields, etc. can be thought of as special kinds of objects that instead of running "methods" have "events". In the same way that a method is a function or a subroutine that runs whenever called from within a program, an "event" is a subroutine that runs whenever a user interaction triggers that event. For example, each button on a form has a "Click" event that runs whenever a user clicks on the button.

To create a new UserForm press ALT-F11 to open the VBA editor. In the Project explorer window (top left side), right-click on the project then select Insert - UserForm. Double check to make sure it is named UserForm1 in the properties window. You can drag command button icons to your new UserForm.

If you're going to change the name of a button, command box, etc. do so right away. If you write hundreds of lines of code and then decide to change the name you will have to go through your entire code and change every individual instance of the name yourself as it will not do so automatically.

To create a new form click Insert > UserForm. If it is not visible select View > Toolbox from the main menu. UserForms will be discussed in more detail in the workshops at the end of the book.

Workshop 7: Using Forms in CATIA VBA

To learn more about creating and using UserForms, please proceed to the back of the book and work through Workshop 7.

WORKSHOP 7

Using Forms in CATIA VBA

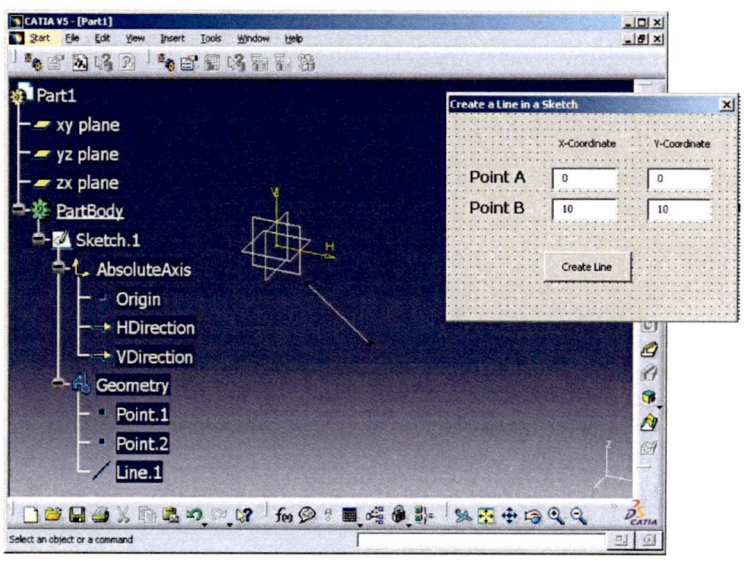

Workshop 7 – Introduction

■ **Description**

In this workshop you will learn how to use VBA forms in order to provide users with a user interface from which they can launch CATIA VBA programs.

■ **Outline**

1. Create a form in the macro library

2. Create various buttons and fields in the form.

3. Re-use code from an earlier workshop in order to add CATIA functionality and interactivity

Step 1a: Create a new form in the macro library

- Open the CATIA VBA editor so that the myVBA macro library is visible. Make sure the "Create_Sketch_01" module is present.

- Right-click on the macro library and select "Insert > UserForm"

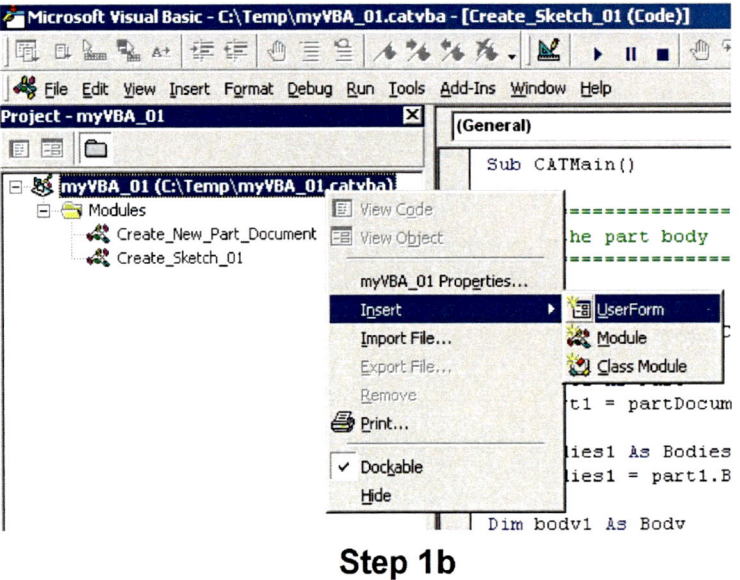

Step 1b

- Name it the form "frmCreateLine" by editing the "(Name)" property.

- Edit the caption of the form by using the "Caption" property.

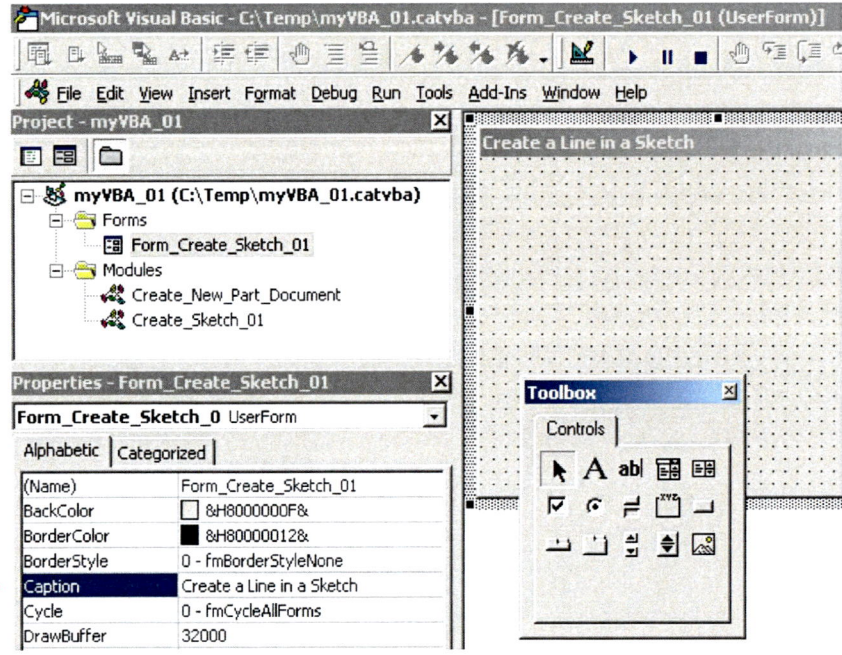

98

Step 2: View the Code of the Form

- With "frmCreateLine" selected in the project tree, click the "View Code" button"

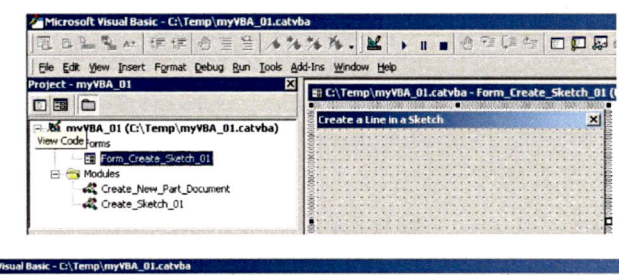

- Note that a code window appears. There are two drop-down menus, one that shows which object's code you are looking at, the other showing the "event" subroutine you are editing. By default the "Click" event is being edited, and the subroubtine for this object and event is "UserForm_Click".

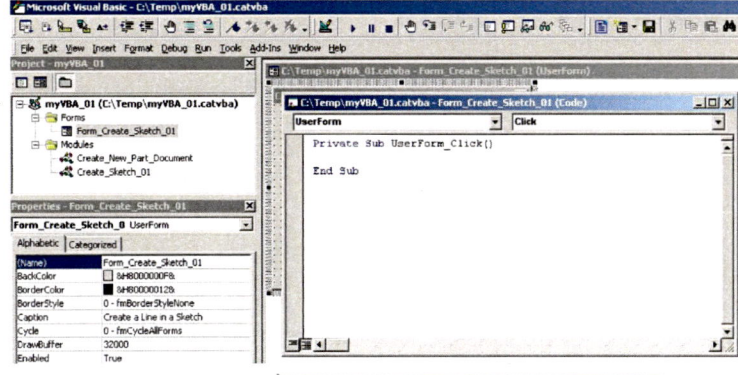

- As a quick experiment, enter the command featured to the right in this "Click"

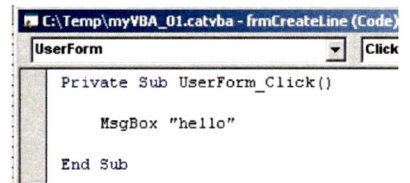

Step 3a: View the Code of the Form

- You need to create a module that displays the form you just created. Create the new module and name it "Show_CreateLine_Form"

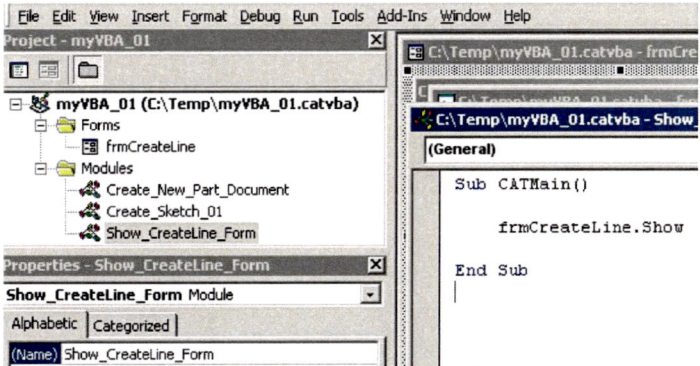

- In the blank code window for the newly created module enter the following code:

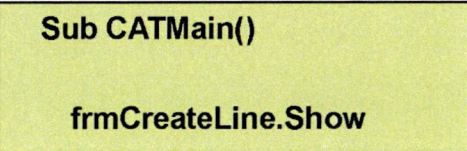

```
Sub CATMain()

frmCreateLine.Show
```

Step 3b: View the Code of the Form

Run this new macro using the "Run" button. A blank form should appear over the CATIA window. Click on the form with your mouse and a message box should appear displaying "hello". As you can see, the form recognizes the click "event" and it runs the code each time you click it. Close the form by using the "x" button in the top right corner.

Step 4: Create a Text Box

- Return to the form in the VBA editor, left-click and hold on the "TextBox" button of the form toolbar, and drag and drop a TextBox onto the form.

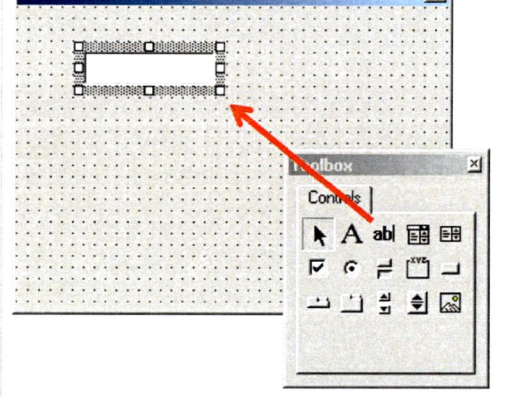

- Click the "View Code" button to view the code of the form. Note that in the drop-down menu on the left, there are now two "objects" to select from "UserForm" and "TextBox1". Each of these objects as it"s own set of "events" that can be chosen from the drop-down menu on the right.

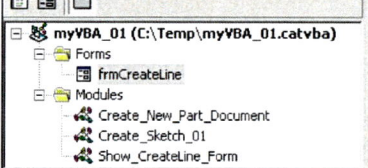

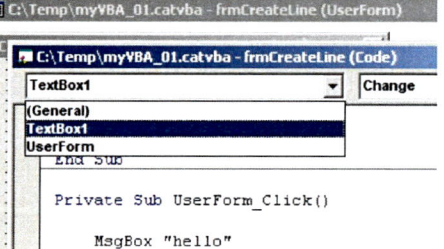

Step 5: Create a Text Box (continued)

- Edit the "(Name)" property of the TextBox to "tbPointA"

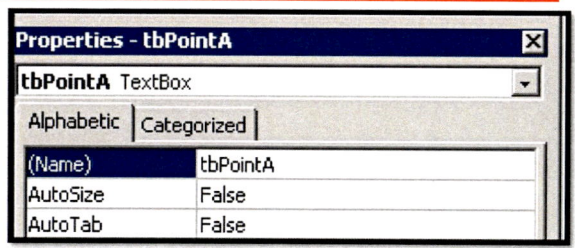

- Edit the "Text" property of the TextBox to be "0" (zero). This will set the TextBox so that it"s default text that it contains is "0".

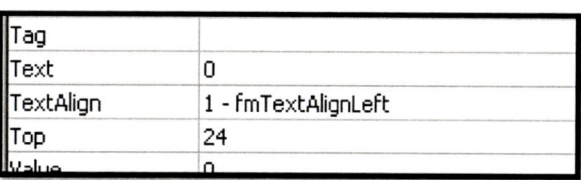

- Edit the code of the Click event of the form like so.

- Note that in the edited code above, tbPointA is an "object" whose "Text" property is being accessed. So the message box will display the contents of the TextBox when the form is clicked.

Private Sub UserForm_Click()

MsgBox tbPointA.Text

End Sub

Step 5: Create a Text Box (continued)

- Run the "Show_CreateLine_Form" Macro

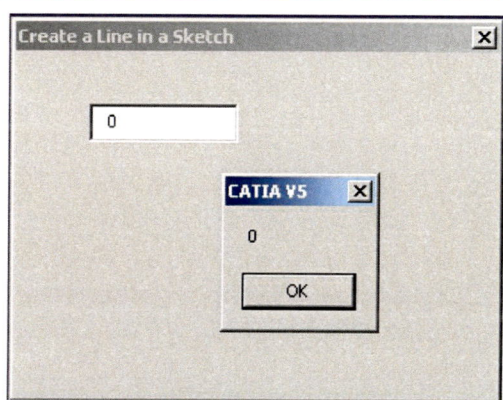

- Click on the form to trigger its Click event. Note that the message box displays the content of the text box.

- Edit the content of the TextBox and click on the form again. Note that the value that gets displayed again matches the content of the TextBox.

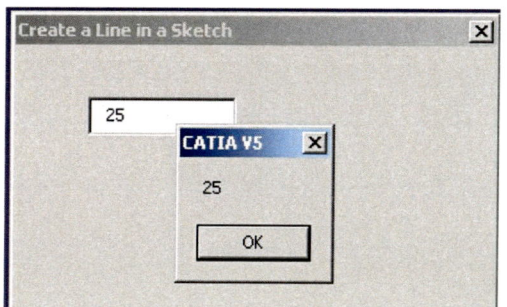

Step 6: Add More Form Objects

- Drag and drop the objects pictured below onto the form. Edit their properties as indicated.

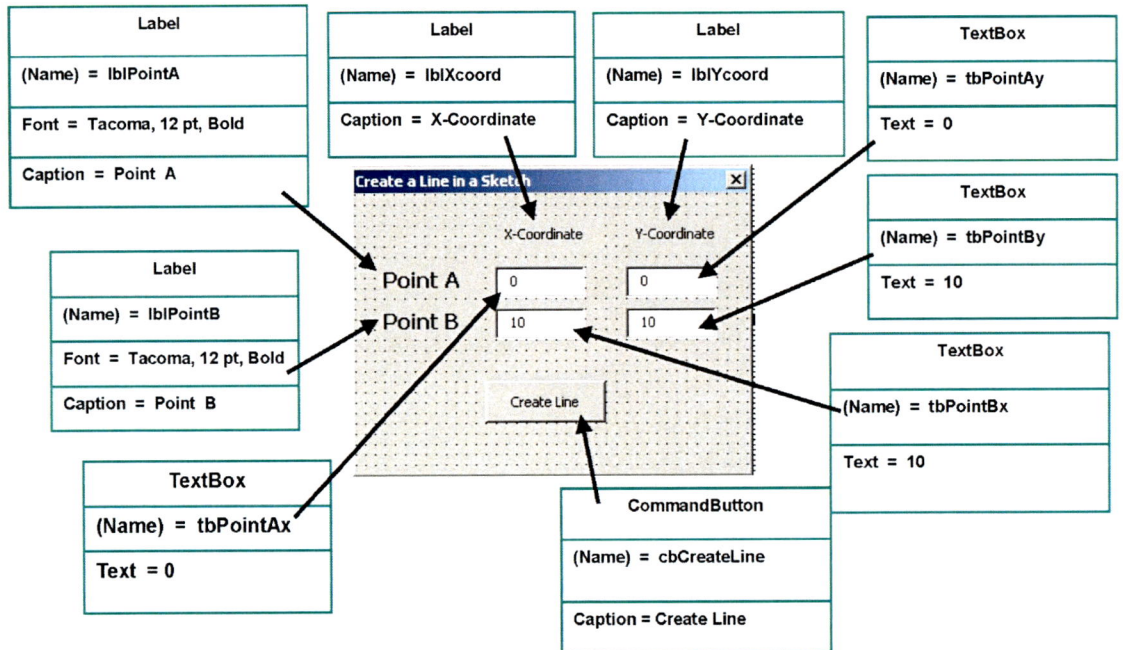

Label	
(Name) = lblPointA	
Font = Tacoma, 12 pt, Bold	
Caption = Point A	

Label	
(Name) = lblXcoord	
Caption = X-Coordinate	

Label	
(Name) = lblYcoord	
Caption = Y-Coordinate	

TextBox	
(Name) = tbPointAy	
Text = 0	

TextBox	
(Name) = tbPointBy	
Text = 10	

Label	
(Name) = lblPointB	
Font = Tacoma, 12 pt, Bold	
Caption = Point B	

TextBox	
(Name) = tbPointBx	
Text = 10	

TextBox	
(Name) = tbPointAx	
Text = 0	

CommandButton	
(Name) = cbCreateLine	
Caption = Create Line	

Step 7: Edit the "Click" Event of the Command Button

- Double-click the "Create Line" command button on the form.

- The code window will come up with various subroutines visible. The cursor should be blinking within the cbCreateLine_Click() subroutine.

- Also, note that because the cursor is positioned in this subroutine, the object and event that are shown in the drop-down menus match this.

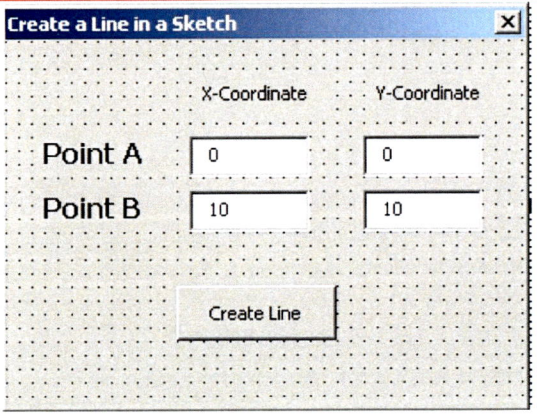

```
Private Sub cbCreateLine_Click()

End Sub

Private Sub TextBox1_Change()

End Sub


Private Sub UserForm_Click()

    MsgBox tbPointA.Value

End Sub
```

9a. Insert the Code from the "Create_Sketch_01"

Rather than redevelop code that creates a line in a sketch, we'll just cut and paste the code previously developed into the Click event of this form. Double-click the "Create_Sketch_01" module to bring its code window up. Select all the code in the code window (other than the "Sub CATMain()" at the beginning and "End Sub" at the end" and hit Ctrl + C.

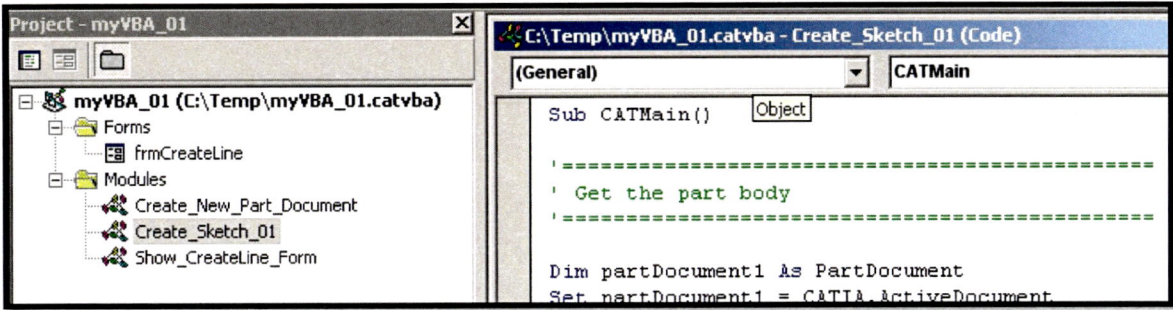

9b. Insert the Code from the "Create_Sketch_01"

- Double-click on "frmCreateLine" on the project tree to bring up the form.

- Double click on the "Create Line" button to bring up the form's code window

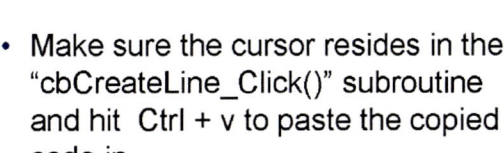

- Make sure the cursor resides in the "cbCreateLine_Click()" subroutine and hit Ctrl + v to paste the copied code in.

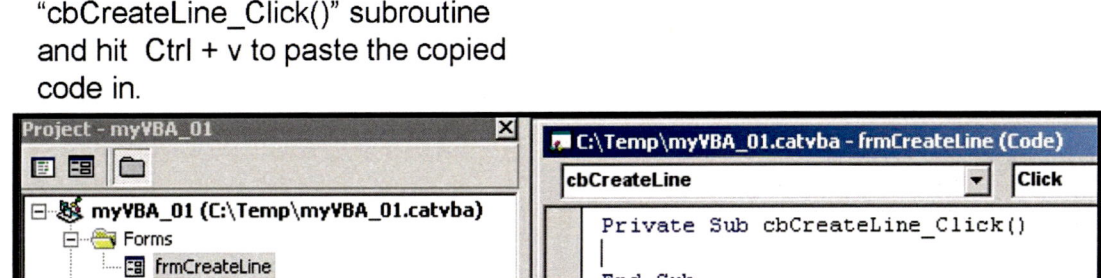

103

Step 10. Edit the Pasted CodeStep

The goal is to edit the code that has been pasted so that when the "Create Line" button is clicked, a line get"s created whose start point has the coordinates of "Point A" and whose end point has the coordinates of "Point B"

The arrows below show the correspondence between the fields of the form and the parameters of the methods that are called in the code.

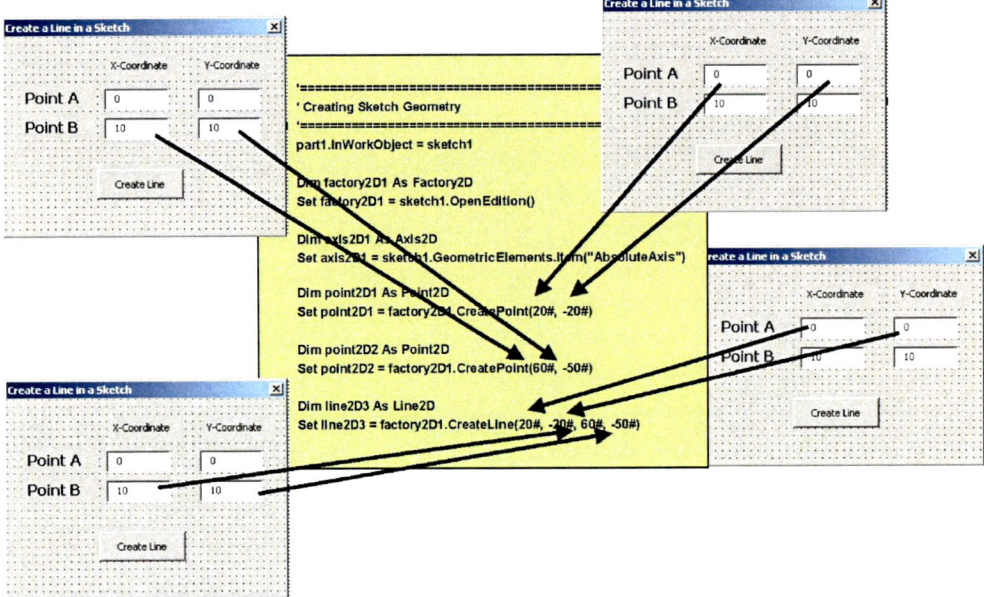

Step 10. Edit the Pasted CodeStep (cont.)

The following replacements need to be made. Note that previously, numerical values were "hard coded" in as parameters to the "CreatePoint" methods. Now we are replacing them with the properties of form objects, in this case the "Text" property of the various TextBox objects that are on the form.

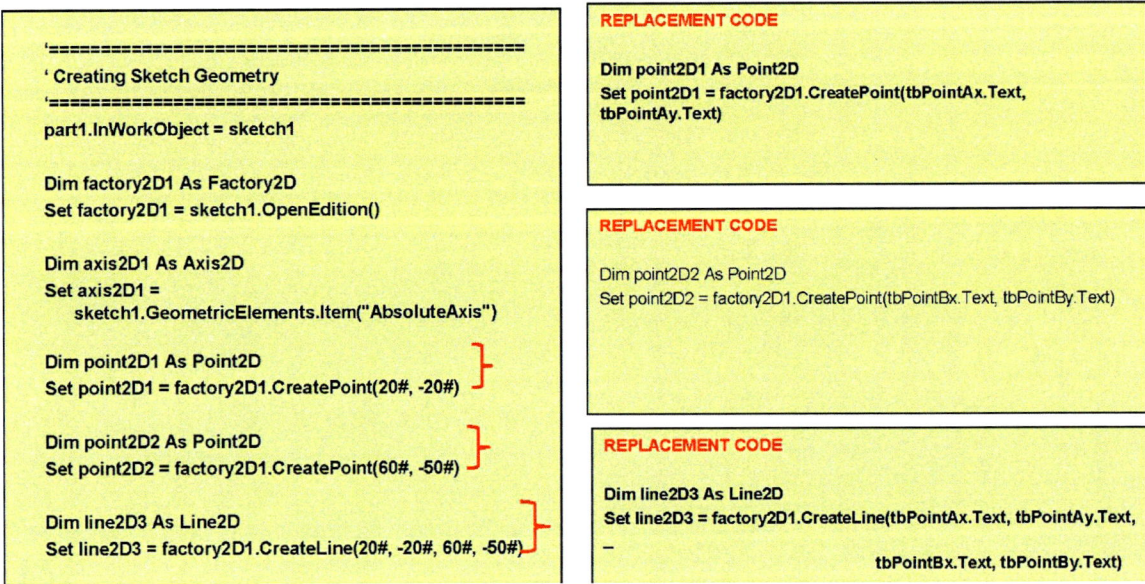

Step 11. Save the VBA project and run the macro

- Highlight the VBA library on the project tree and save your changes.

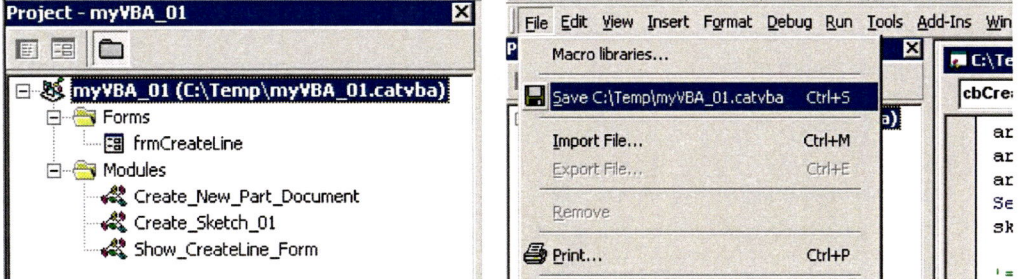

- Close the VBA window, open a new part, and open the macros dialog through Tools > Macro > Macros, and run the "Show_CreateLine_Form" macro.

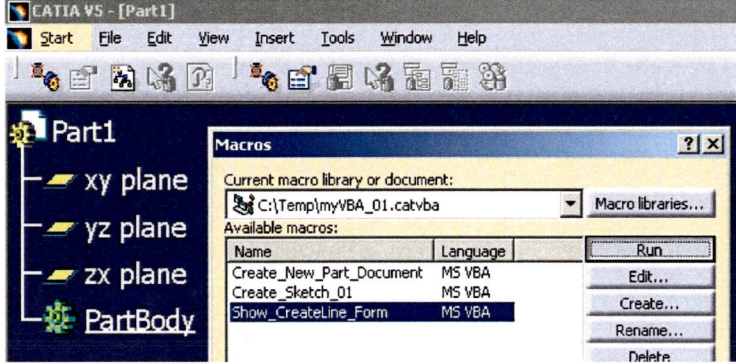

Step 12a. Create a sketch using the form

- Click the "Create Line" button and you will see that a sketch appears containing a line whose coordinates match those that are in the form TextBox objects. However, the form remains open, and if you attempt to interact with CATIA you are unable because the form has been shown in what is called "modal" mode. It would be nice to change this so that after a sketch is created, you could zoom in or rotate, expand the spec tree, etc.

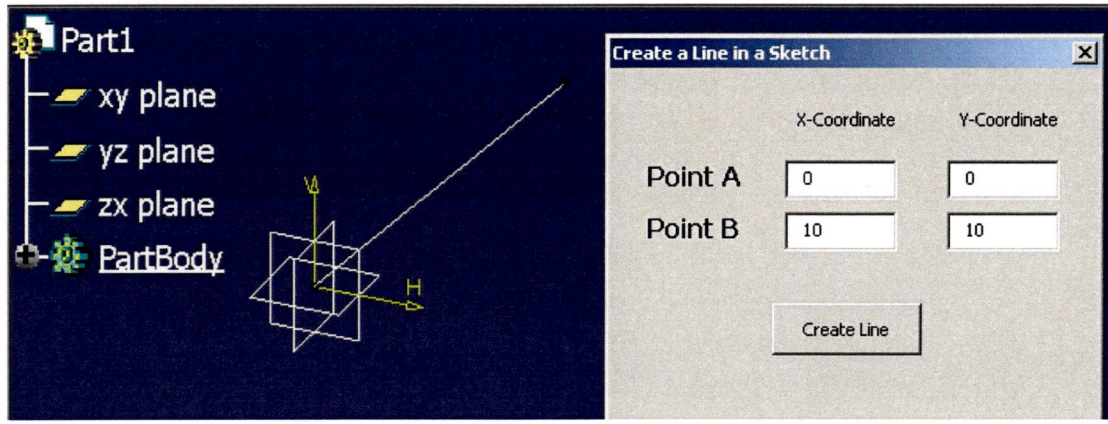

Step 12b. Create a sketch using the form

- Open the VBA editor and navigate to the "Show_CreateLine_Form" module and edit it as show below. Note that an argument "vbModeless" will be passed to the "Show" subroutine that is called on the form.

```
Sub CATMain()


    frmCreateLine.Show vbModeless


End Sub
```

- Save the project, close the VBA editor, and run the "Show_CreateLine_Form" macro. Note that even before you hit the "Create Line" button you are able to interact with CATIA (zoom in, rotate, etc.). Change point coordinate values on the form and hit the "Create Line" button to create another sketch.

Workshop 7 – Conclusion

This concludes Workshop 7. In this workshop you have learned to:

- Create a form and insert code into it"s "Event" subroutines

- Add form objects to the form such as TextBox objects, Label objects, and CommandButton objects, edit their properties, and insert code into their events as well

- Reference the properties of form objects for use in code. For instance, you used the "Text" properties of the TextBox objects that were created on the form.

- "Show" a form in both "Modal" and "Modeless" scenarios

Visit www.scripting4v5.com for more articles, examples, and downloadable CATScript files.

Chapter 7: Drafting

CATIA's drafting workbench features two basic types of grouping all 2D features: **Generative Drafting** takes the 3D CATIA objects and represents them in 2D views within a drawing while **Interactive Drafting** represents 2D features directly created in the 2D views with no 3D data associated with it. The **DrawingDocument** object aggregates a **DrawingSheets** collection. Each **DrawingSheet** of this collection aggregates a **DrawingViews** collection.

A drawing contains at least two views: the background view and the Main View. That is the view in which you can draw just after creating a drawing. **The ActiveSheet**: The active sheet can be found in the DrawingSheets collection. **The ActiveView** can be found in the DrawingViews collection

A **DrawingView** can be the "Front View" or another view relative to the "Front View".**DrawingViewGenerativeBehavior** can define both behavior: **DefineFrontView()** defines the "Front View" and its direction. **DefineProjectionView()** defines another view relative to the "Front View" Other methods allow creating other types of views such as Section Views, Detail Views, etc. **Generative Views** – *DrawingView* owns a "**document**" property that allows you to specify the associated 3D document from which the "generative view" is created.

- **Interactive Views** – *DrawingView* owns a "**Factory2D**" property that allows you to create 2D features. This kind of view is called an "Interactive View".
- **Filling the Title block** - The **Texts** collection allows you to create 2D texts in the drawing
- **Extract Dimensions** - A *DrawingShee*t has the method called *GenerateDimension()* that generates dimensions automatically in all the views from the 3D geometry.

There is also a special viewer for Drawings called Viewer2D. The Viewer2D contains many of the same properties and methods of a viewer3D, but it acts upon a CATDrawing document. You can set it the same way as a Viewer3D, but only if the active window contains a CATDrawing. If not, you will get a type mismatch error that you need to use error handling (presented earlier in this text) to trap, otherwise your application might crash.

- **DrawingSheets** is the collection of sheets.
- **DrawingViews** is the collection of views.
- **DrawingViewGeneriveBehavior** is the object responsible for views from 3D models.
- **Factory2D** owns the methods to create non-associative geometry for lines, points...

- **DrawingComponents** contains 2D components.
- **DrawingTexts** is for text annotations.
- **GeometricalElements** is for geometry created by Factory2D.

The process to create drawing views is as follows:

1. Create an empty view
2. Retrieve the GenerativeBehavior object
3. Create the link with the 3D model
4. Set the attributes of the view
5. Define the view
6. Update the view

The steps listed above are followed in the example to create a front view:

```
Sub CATMain()

'create an empty view
     Dim oView As Drawing View
     Set oView = oSheet.View.Add("Front")

'retrieve the generative behavior object
     Dim oGeneral As DrawingViewGenerativeBehavior
     Set oGeneral = oView.GenerativeBehavior

'create the link with the 3D part model

     Dim oPartDoc As PartDocument
     Set oPartDoc = CATIA.Documents.Item("Part1.CATPart")
     oGeneral.Document = oPartDoc.Product

'set the hidden lines to ON
     oGeneral.HiddenLineMode = catHlrModeOn

'create the front view
     oGeneral.DefineFrontView 1, 0, 0, 0, 0, 1

'update the view
     oGeneral.Update

End Sub
```

Create Frames and Title Blocks

Frames and title blocks can be created in Drawings using VBA. Place the frame and title block in the background by activating the back ground view. **Factory2D** is used to draw the frame and title block. The **DrawingRoot** method can be used to get the paper width and height to offset the frame a constant distance from the edges. Follow along with the comments in the example below.

```
Option Explicit
Sub CATMain()

    Dim oDrwDoc As DrawingDocument
    Set oDrwDoc = CATIA.ActiveDocument

'memorize which View was active before the macro
    Dim oViewerActive As DrawingView
    Set oViewerActive = oDrwDoc.DrawingRoot.ActiveSheet.Views.ActiveView

'get the background View
    Dim oView As DrawingView
    Set oView = oDrwDoc.DrawingRoot.ActiveSheet.Views.Item("Background View")
    oView.Activate

'create a Frame
    Dim oFact As Factory2D
    Set oFact = oView.Factory2D
    Dim dW As Double
    dW = oDrwDoc.DrawingRoot.ActiveSheet.GetPaperWidth
    Dim dH As Double
    dH = oDrwDoc.DrawingRoot.ActiveSheet.GetPaperHeight
    Dim oLine As Line2D

'draw the frame 10 units in from the edges of the paper
    Set oLine = oFact.CreateLine(10#, 10#, dW - 10#, 10#)
    Set oLine = oFact.CreateLine(dW - 10#, 10#, dW - 10#, dH - 10#)
    Set oLine = oFact.CreateLine(dW - 10#, dH - 10#, 10#, dH - 10#)
    Set oLine = oFact.CreateLine(10#, dH - 10#, 10#, 10#)

'text objects are used to write notes on the drawing
    Dim oNote As DrawingText
    Set oNote = oView.Texts.Add(" ", 100#, 100#)
    oNote.Text = "GENERAL NOTES - UNLESS OTHERWISE SPECIFIED"
    oNote.Text = oNote.Text & vbCrLf & "1. Dimensions are mm"
    oNote.Text = oNote.Text & vbCrLf & "2. Edges to be deburred"
    oNote.AnchorPosition = catTopLeft
    oNote.SetFontSize 0, 0, 3.5
    oNote.WrappingWidth = 200#
```

```
'create the title block as a table
    Dim oTables As DrawingTables
    Set oTables = oView.Tables



    Dim oTable As DrawingTable
    Set oTable = oTables.Add(dW - 360#, 70#, 3#, 3#, 20#, 90#)
    oTable.SetColumnSize 1, 90
    oTable.SetColumnSize 2, 200
    oTable.SetColumnSize 3, 60
    oTable.MergeCells 1, 1, 1, 3
    oTable.SetCellString 1, 1, "TITLE BLOCK"
    oTable.SetCellAlignment 1, 1, CatTableMiddleCenter


    'set the font sizes for each table cell
    oTable.GetCellObject(1, 1).SetFontSize 0, 0, 7
    oTable.GetCellObject(2, 1).SetFontSize 0, 0, 5
    oTable.GetCellObject(3, 1).SetFontSize 0, 0, 5
    oTable.GetCellObject(2, 2).SetFontSize 0, 0, 7
    oTable.GetCellObject(3, 2).SetFontSize 0, 0, 7
    oTable.GetCellObject(2, 3).SetFontSize 0, 0, 5
    oTable.GetCellObject(3, 3).SetFontSize 0, 0, 5

'use the VB date function to display the current date
    oTable.SetCellString 2, 1, "DATE: " & Date
    oTable.SetCellAlignment 2, 1, CatTableMiddleCenter

    oTable.SetCellString 3, 1, "SCALE: 1:" &
oDrwDoc.DrawingRoot.ActiveSheet.Scale
    oTable.SetCellAlignment 3, 1, CatTableMiddleCenter

'use the count property to count the total number of sheets
    oTable.SetCellString 2, 3, "SHEET 1 of " &_
oDrwDoc.DrawingRoot.Sheets.Count
    oTable.SetCellAlignment 2, 3, CatTableMiddleCenter


'link to the part document to displayed the desired properties
    Dim oPrtDoc As PartDocument
    Set oPrtDoc = CATIA.Documents.Item("Part1.CATPart")

'get the front view
    Dim oViewF As DrawingView
    Set oViewF = oDrwDoc.DrawingRoot.ActiveSheet.Views.Item("Front")

    Dim oParent As Product
    Set oParent = oViewF.GenerativeBehavior.Document

'display the part number from the CATPart in the table
    oTable.SetCellString 2, 2, "PART NO: " & oParent.PartNumber
    oTable.SetCellAlignment 2, 2, CatTableMiddleCenter

'display the mass of the part model in the table
```

```
oTable.SetCellString 3, 2, "WEIGHT: " & oParent.Analyze.Mass & "kg"
oTable.SetCellAlignment 3, 2, CatTableMiddleCenter

oView.SaveEdition

'activate the originally active view
oViewerActive.Activate

'update everything in the end
oDrwDoc.DrawingRoot.Update

End Sub
```

Exercise 7.1 Draw a 2D circle in the drafting workbench

Macros cannot be recorded in the drafting workbench so there's no cheating on this exercise. In order to create a sketch of a circle in the drafting workbench, use CreateClosedCircle(x coordinate, y coordinate, radius) . Here are the general steps to follow to successfully complete this exercise:

1. Create a new drawing (paper size is irrelevant).
2. Activate the drawing document.
3. Get the background view.
4. Use Factory2d and CreateClosedCircle to sketch a 2D circle of radius 100 at x=50and y=100 coordinates.

You can find the solution at the back of the book but I highly encourage you to try and figure it out on your own first.

Chapter 8: Parameters, Formulas, and Relations

Many times a VB application is developed to create, read, or modify Parameters. Each type of CATIA document contains a Parameters and Relations collection. Parameters are all accessed from the "Parameters" collection of a part:

```
Dim oParameters As Parameters
Set oParameters = oPart.Parameters
```

To create a length parameter:

```
Dim oParm As Parameter
Set oParm=oParameters.CreateDimension("Name","Length",10.0)
```

Other parameter types can also be created including **CreateBoolean**, **CreateString**, and **CreateReal**.

To read a parameter named "PartName":

```
Dim oParam As Parameter
Set oParam = oPart.Parameters.Item("PartName")
```

To display a parameter value in mm (regardless of what the units are set to):

```
Msgbox oParam.Value
```

There are multiple ways to call access to a parameter value. **ValueAsString** returns the value of a parameter as a string and includes the current system of units. To display a parameter value in the current units:

```
MsgBox oParam.ValueAsString
```

ValuateFromString sets a value to the parameter and you have to pass it the units in the string. To set a parameter dimension to a value of 4 inches:

```
oParam.ValuateFromString("4in")
```

Parameters in CATIA V5 are virtually useless and simply take up space in the tree unless they are linked to something else. A link between a parameter and a piece of geometry is called a relation. There is a collection of relations in each part:

```
Dim oRel As Relations
Set oRel = oPart.Relations
```

Relations can be found by searching for a specific name:

```
Dim oRel As Relation
Set oRel = oPart.Relations.Item("RelationName")
```

To create a relation use CreateFormula(name of relation, comment, driven object, driving parameter):

```
'parameter name is ZZZ will drive point's x-coordinate
Dim oRel As Relation
Set oRelations.CreateFormula("ZRel", " ", oPoint.X, "ZZZ")
'must always update the part when a new parameter or relation is made
oPart.Update
```

Other methods of relations include CreateDesignTable, CreateHorizontalDesignTable, Item, and Remove. An appropriate license is required if trying to create Relations other than formulas or design tables (such as KWA, KWE, or PEO).

Constraints

To get the constraints collections from a product use the following code:

```
Dim oConst As Constraints
Set oConst = oProd.Connections("CATIAConstraints")
```

The following methods can then be used:

- **AddMonoEltCst**: constraint for one geometrical element
- **AddBiEltCst**: constraint for two elements
- **AddTriEltCst**: constraint for three elements
- **Remove**: remove a constraint

Adding constraints in sketches was discussed earlier in the sketching section. To create a fix together constraint between multiple parts or products, first retrieve the collection then use the Add method to actually create it, like so:

```
Dim oFixTogether As FixTogethers
Set = oFixTogether = oRootProd.Connections("CATIAFixTogethers")

Dim fix1 As FixTogether
Set fix1 = oFixTogther.Add()
```

Measurement Macros

The measurement tools in CATIA V5 ("Measure Item" & "Measure Between") have not yet been exposed by Dassault Systèmes, but there are other workaround methods to do measurements using the CATIA Object Model. The first way is to use a parameter and the "measure" tools which are a part of the formula editor in V5. This can be done by using the parameter and reference interfaces that we looked at earlier. The only difference is that the "measure" functions are input as the driving argument in the CreateFormula method. For example, to create a parameter that will measure the distance between two points, called "MyEndPt1" and "MyEndPt2" you would use:

```
Dim objDistance As Parameter
Set objDistance = Parms.CreateDimension("Distance","LENGTH", 0)

Dim objDistanceRel As Relation

Set objDistanceRel = _
Part.Relations.CreateFormula("DistanceForm", "", _
myDistance,_        "distance(`Geometrical        Set.1\MyEndPt1`,`Geometrical_
Set.1\MyEndPt2`)")

MsgBox "The endpoints are " & myDistance.ValueAsString & " apart."
```

Another method to measure elements is with the DMU workbench properties and methods. This requires a license of DMU. Without the license, the calls will not work. Examples of how to use these DMU programming objects can be found in the CATIA On-Line documentation for automation.

Changing Units and other Tools >Options

The settings under the Tools>Options menu can be changed with a macro, such as automatically changing the units from inch to mm. This is useful if you need have another code that needs the units set to metric or English in order to run properly. The first lines of code from CATIA Change Units.CATScript are:

```
Dim oSettingControllers As SettingControllers
Set oSettingControllers = CATIA.SettingControllers
Dim oUnitsSheetSettingAtt As SettingController
Set oUnitsSheetSettingAtt =
oSettingControllers.Item("CATLieUnitsSheetSettingCtrl")
```

The SettingControllers manages the parameters available in the property pages of the Tools > Options menus. Each parameter setting may be represented by one or several attributes in the underlying setting repository.

All setting controllers share the five methods of the SettingController object to deal with the whole set, or a subset of the setting attributes:

- **Commit** to make a memory copy of the setting attribute values
- **Rollback** to restore the last memory copy of the setting attribute values
- **ResetToAdminValues** to restore the administered values of all the attributes
- **ResetToAdminValuesByName** to restore the administered values of a subset of the attributes
- **SaveRepository** to make a persistent copy of the setting attribute values on file

You may have also noticed the code with **UnitSheetSetting** which is the interface to be used to read or modify the CATIA\Tools\Options settings for values of Units. The next part of the change units macro:

```
Dim oMagnitude as String
oMagnitude = "LENGTH"
Dim oUnit as String
oUnit = ""
Dim oGetDecimal as Double
Dim oGetExpo as Double
oUnitsSheetSettingAtt.GetMagnitudeValues oMagnitude, oUnit, oGetDecimal,
oGetExpo
If (oUnit = "Inch") Then
Dim oUnitInch as String
oUnitInch = "Millimeter"
oUnitsSheetSettingAtt.SetMagnitudeValues _
oMagnitude, oUnitInch, 6.000000, 3.000000
oUnitsSheetSettingAtt.SaveRepositoryForUnits()
oUnitsSheetSettingAtt.CommitForUnits()
oUnitsSheetSettingAtt.Commit()
MsgBox "The Current Unit is now: " & oUnitInch
End If
```

Here you can see where you use Commit and how it comes into play. Commit saves the current values of the setting attributes managed by the setting controller in a specific memory area. Successive calls to Commit overwrite the memory area. The values saved by the last call to Commit can be restored from that memory area using the Rollback method.

Magnitude is where you set the type of unit you want to change, in our case "Length" (as opposed to Angle, Time, Mass, etc.). Next, set the units to Millimeter or Inch. The numbers are then to set the exponential notation for values greater than 10e+/-.

Chapter 9: Positioning Components

There are two main ways to manipulate the position of a "component" (child part, child assembly, child component):

1. The methods GetComponents and SetComponents methods of the Position object.
2. The "Apply" method of the Move object.

All of these methods deal with twelve member Variant arrays. The CATIA programming API's use arrays of twelve numbers to describe a child axis-system in a parent coordinate space

Absolute Positioning versus 3D Transformations

The SetPosition method on the Product object is used for ABSOLUTE positioning of a component relative to the parent axis system. The Move object and its Apply method are used to perform rotations and translations on the child axis system, RELATIVE to the parent axis system. The following code shows how to get the position matrix of a child component of an assembly. Note that there are some strange conventions that must be adhered to:

```
Dim prod1 As Product
'Assume prod1 gets set here
Set prod1nd = prod1
Dim pos1(11)
prod1nd.Position.GetComponents pos1
```

Although the Product object was set, a non-dimmed variable "prod1nd" must be set to this product, and this one must be used instead of "prod1". The array "pos1" is dimmed without a type, which causes it to be an array of variants.

Assume that the component on which this code is run is positioned such that its axis system is ORIENTED the same as its parent, but it is positioned in its parent's coordinate system 1000 mm along the x- direction and 500 mm along the y-direction. The x-axis, the y-axis, and the z-axis are all oriented in the "default" fashion.

The pos1 array would then contain these values:

```
pos1(0) = 1.0
pos1(1) = 0.0
pos1(2) = 0.0

pos1(3) = 0.0
pos1(4) = 1.0
pos1(5) = 0.0

pos1(6) = 0.0
pos1(7) = 0.0
pos1(8) = 1.0

pos1(9) = 1000.0   'x-coordinate of the origin in the parent coordinate space
pos1(10) = 500.0   'y-coordinate of the origin in the parent coordinate space
pos1(11) = 0.0     'z-coordinate of the origin in the parent coordinate space
```

The SetComponents method on the Position object works to set the absolute position of the child component in the parent's coordinate space. Relative to the orientation shown on the previous example, these values will have the same effect on the position of the component as if it were rotated 90 degrees about the z-axis.

```
Dim prod1 As Product
Set prod1 = CATIA.ActiveDocument.Product
Set prod1nd = prod1
Dim pos1(11)

pos1(0) = 0.0
pos1(1) = 1.0
pos1(2) = 0.0

pos1(3) = -1.0
pos1(4) =  0.0
pos1(5) =  0.0

pos1(6) = 0.0
pos1(7) = 0.0
pos1(8) = 1.0

pos1(9) =  0.0    'x-coordinate of the origin in the parent coordinate space
pos1(10) = 0.0    'y-coordinate of the origin in the parent coordinate space
pos1(11) = 0.0    'z-coordinate of the origin in the parent coordinate space

prod1nd.Position.SetComponents pos1
```

The Move Object

The Move object only serves to perform "transformations" on the child component, also relative to its parent's coordinate space. These transformations are described by numerical values stored in a variant array, which is passed as an argument to the "Apply" method. The following definition for moveArray, used in the code below, would have the effect of translating the component 1000 units along the direction of its parent's coordinate space.

```
Dim prod1 As Product
Set prod1 = CATIA.ActiveDocument
Set prod1nd = prod1

Dim moveArray(11)

moveArray(0)  = 1.0
moveArray(1)  = 0.0
moveArray(2)  = 0.0

moveArray(3)  = 0.0
moveArray(4)  = 1.0
moveArray(5)  = 0.0

moveArray(6)  = 0.0
moveArray(7)  = 0.0
moveArray(8)  = 1.0

moveArray(9)  = 1000.0    'Distance to move the product in the x-direction
moveArray(10) = 0.0       'Distance to move the product in the y-direction
moveArray(11) = 0.0       'Distance to move the product in the z-direction

prod1nd.Move.Apply moveArray
```

Rotation Matrices

The numbers that are used to define the variant array that is passed into the "Apply" method of the Move object need to be derived from the values that are calculated in these rotation matrices.

$$R_x(\theta) = \begin{bmatrix} 1 & 0 & 0 \\ 0 & \cos\theta & -\sin\theta \\ 0 & \sin\theta & \cos\theta \end{bmatrix}$$

$$R_y(\theta) = \begin{bmatrix} \cos\theta & 0 & \sin\theta \\ 0 & 1 & 0 \\ -\sin\theta & 0 & \cos\theta \end{bmatrix}$$

$$R_z(\theta) = \begin{bmatrix} \cos\theta & -\sin\theta & 0 \\ \sin\theta & \cos\theta & 0 \\ 0 & 0 & 1 \end{bmatrix}$$

Rotation about the X-Axis

As an example, here is how the values of a rotation-about-x matrix map to the array that needs to be used with the Apply method of the Move object.

$$R_x(\theta) = \begin{bmatrix} 1 & 0 & 0 \\ 0 & \cos\theta & -\sin\theta \\ 0 & \sin\theta & \cos\theta \end{bmatrix}$$

moveArray(0) = 1
moveArray(1) = 0
moveArray(2) = 0

$$R_x(\theta) = \begin{bmatrix} 1 & 0 & 0 \\ 0 & \cos\theta & -\sin\theta \\ 0 & \sin\theta & \cos\theta \end{bmatrix}$$

moveArray(3) = 0
moveArray(4) = cos THETA
moveArray(5) = sin THETA

moveArray(6) = 0
moveArray(7) = -sin THETA
moveArray(8) = cos THETA

$$R_x(\theta) = \begin{bmatrix} 1 & 0 & 0 \\ 0 & \cos\theta & -\sin\theta \\ 0 & \sin\theta & \cos\theta \end{bmatrix}$$

moveArray(9) = 0
moveArray(10) = 0
moveArray(11) = 0

120

Suggested use of Move and Apply

With all of this in mind, for most programming tasks, if the Move object needs to be used to manipulate the position of a component of an assembly, it is easiest to define multiple subroutines, such as

```
Sub RotateAboutX( prod1 As Product, X As Double)

Sub RotateAboutY( prod1 As Product, Y As Double)

Sub RotateAboutZ( prod1 As Product, Z As Double)

Sub Translate(prod1 As Product,xDir As Double, yDir As Double,zDir As Double)
```

This way, you can apply the transformations in the order that they need to be applied in.

Chapter 10: Importing and Exporting Data

CATIA V5 running on Windows can be automated with any application that can connect to Windows Component Object Model (COM), including VBA (Excel, Word, CATIA, etc.), VBScript, JavaScript, Visual Basic 6.0, Microsoft Developers Studio.NET, and others. Data can be imported and exported from CATIA to other software applications. The macro can run in either CATIA or the Microsoft Office application. This text will cover exporting to images, exporting BOM, and export to Microsoft Excel, PowerPoint, and Word though it is certainly not limited to these alone.

Application is the root object for all CATIA macros. To launch CATIA from another application, such as Visual Basic, and CATIA is already running:

```
Dim CATIAV5 As Object
Set CATIAV5 = GetObject(, "CATIA.Application")
```

The GetObject will fail if the application is not already running. Therefore, error handling should be used or, alternatively, you can launch a brand new application every time using CreateObject:

```
'This macro will start CATIA

Dim CATIAV5 As Object
Set CATIA = CreateObject("CATIA.Application")
CATIA.Visible = True
```

Please note, if there are multiple versions of CATIA, the CreateObject will launch the current registered version only. See the appendix to learn how to register a different version of CATIA.

Export Images

The viewer discussed earlier gives you the capability of exporting the 3D window into a JPG picture format:

```
objViewer3D.CaptureToFile(catCaptureFormatJPEG,"C:\myPicture.jpg")
```

Other available formats:

1. BMP
2. TIFF
3. CGM
4. EMF
5. TIFFGreyScale

The code below show you how to save the CATIA capture file as .png . Or you can save it as TIFF, BMP, or JPEG if you want to by changing the number in this line of code or by adding your own file extension to the name (.png, .bmp).

```
Dim fileloc, Exten, Strname As String
      Fileloc="C:\Screen Capture\"
      Exten = ".png"
      Strname = fileloc & partName & exten
Objviewer3D.Capturetofile 4, strname
```

The size of the picture is, by default, the size of the active window. You can change the size of the picture with this code:

```
Set window=CATIA.ActiveWindow
      H=win.Height
      W=win.Width
      sLF=Chr(10)
      win.Height=InputBox("Enter height, reference is upper _
      left hand corner", "Change height", win.height)
          If win.Height="" Then
      Exit Sub
End If
```

Then do the same thing for the width and restore original settings at the end.

Export BOM

A bill of material (BOM) for an assembly can be exported to a text file.

```
Sub CATMain()
      'create a new product document
Dim oProdDoc As ProductDocument
Set oProdDoc = CATIA.Documents.Add("Product")
      'retrieve the products collection for the root product
      Dim oRootProd As Product
      Set oRootProd = oProdDoc.Product
      'extract the BOM
```

```
      Dim response As Integer

      Response = MsgBox("Extract BOM?", vbYesNo, "Extract BOM")

            If Response = vbYes Then

      oRootProd.ExtractBOM CATFileTypeText, "C:\User\BOM.txt"
End If
oRootProd.Update
End Sub
```

Export the Specification Tree

Sometimes you may need to quickly export the specification tree to a text or Excel file. The following example uses an input box asking the user to select whether he wants to export as either an .xls or .txt file type.

```
Language="VBSCRIPT"
Sub CATMain()

Dim productDocument1 As Document
Set productDocument1 = CATIA.ActiveDocument

'Input box to select txt or xls
Dim exportFormat As String
exportFormat = Inputbox ("Please choose format to export the tree as._
Type either 'xls' or 'txt'")

IF exportFormat <> "xls" THEN

IF exportFormat <> "txt" THEN

MsgBox "Did not enter txt or xls. Program cancelled, please retry macro."

Else

'Input box to enter name of file
Dim partName As String
partName = Inputbox ("Please enter the file name.")

'Input box to enter file location
Dim oLocation As String
oLocation = "C:\Macro Files\"
productDocument1.ExportData oLocation & partName & "." & exportFormat, "txt"

End If
End If
End Sub
```

Export to Microsoft Excel

Spreadsheets are used in the world of engineering to create part lists and bills of material. These are typically created in Microsoft Excel. A macro can be created to export data from CATIA into an Excel spreadsheet, quickly automating this process. First, make sure the Microsoft Office references (type libraries) have been registered.

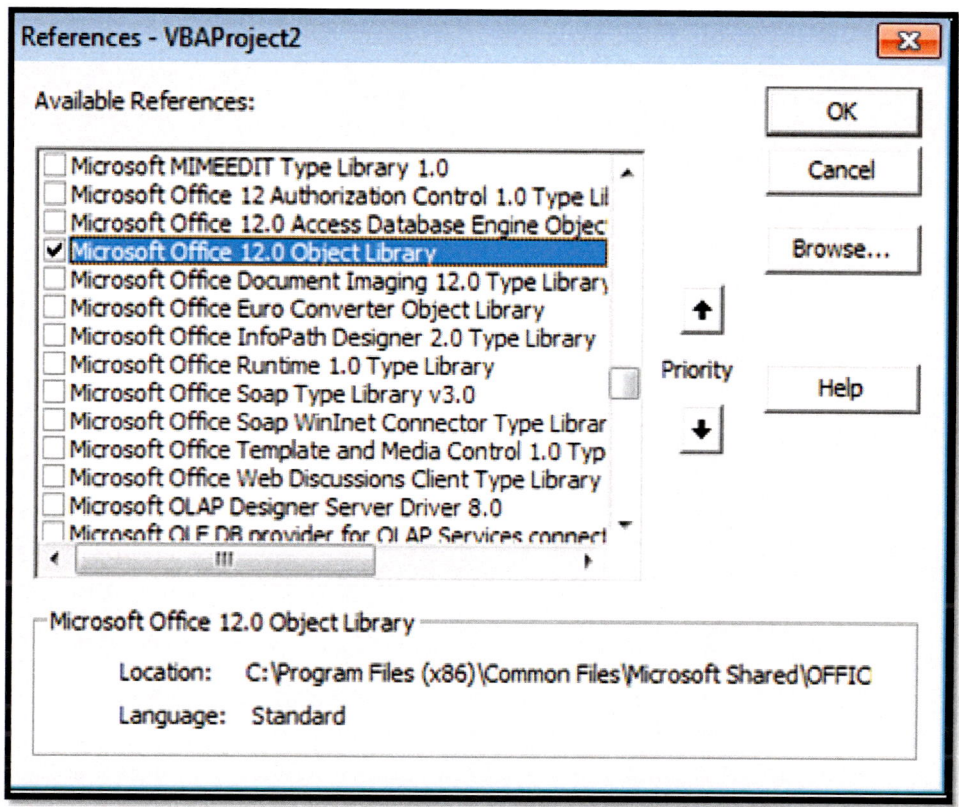

Before launching Excel we need to declare all of our objects and variables including the Microsoft Excel application itself, each workbook, each worksheet within each workbook, etc.

```
Dim Excel As Object
Dim workbooks As workbooks
Dim workbook As workbook
Dim Sheets As Object
Dim Sheet As Object
Dim worksheet As Excel.worksheet
Dim myworkbook As Excel.workbook
Dim myworksheet As Excel.worksheet
Set workbooks = Excel.Application.workbooks
```

```
Set myworkbook = Excel.workbooks.Add
Set myworksheet = Excel.ActiveWorkbook.Add
Set myworksheet = Excel.Sheets.Add
```

Launching Excel from CATIA

There are several methods to go about launching the Microsoft Excel program from within CATIA. One method forces the user to close any open Excel files before running the macro through error handling:

```
On Error Resume Next

        Set Excel = GetObject(, "EXCEL.Application")
        If Err.Number <> 0 Then
        Err.Clear
        Set Excel = CreateObject("EXCEL.Application")
    Else
        Err.Clear

MsgBox "Please note you have to close Excel", vbCritical

        Exit Sub
    End If
```

Or, we may just want to create a new worksheet and not make the user have to close Excel first (which is more user friendly), thus we will use this preferred code:

```
On Error Resume Next

        Set Excel = GetObject(, "EXCEL.Application")
        If Err.Number <> 0 Then

        Err.Clear
        Set Excel = CreateObject("Excel.Application")

    End If
```

Screen Updating and Excel Visibility

When you do not want to see your screen follow the actions of your VBA procedure (macro), you start and end your code with the following sentences:

At the start:
```
Application.ScreenUpdating = False
```

Then at the end:
```
Application.ScreenUpdating = True 'make Excel visible
```

126

To display your completed Excel file, type this line of code at the point in your program when you want Excel to appear.

```
Excel.Visible = True
```

Entering Cell Values

To write text in a specific cell, such as the first row's header values, use Excel.Cell (row #, column #).

```
'row one header
'Cell A1
Excel.Cells(1,1)="Part Number"
'Cell B1
Excel.Cells(1,2)="Fasteners"
Excel.Cells(1,3)="Name"
```

You can use a variable to assign a cell number. For example, if you have a For Loop and want the Excel row number to increase by one for each iteration of the loop you might use this:

```
Dim RwNum As Integer
        For I = 1 to 10

        Excel.Cells(RwNum, 4) = getThickness
        Excel.Cells(RwNum, 5) = getMaterial
        Excel.Cells(RwNum, 6) = getMass
        RwNum = RwNum + 1

        Next 'i
```

Here is an example using an IF THEN formula. If the name of the CATIA document does not equal PERMANENT_FASTENERS then enter the name of the document and add one to the row count, otherwise enter no cell value and leave the row count the same. "Namebody" is the name of a body within a catpart.

```
If namebody <>"PERMANENT_FASTENERS" Then
        Excel.Cells(RwNum+1,2)= namebody
        RwNum = RwNum + 1
    End If
Else
RwNum = RwNum
```

Excel Formulas

You may also need to include formulas to attain the correct cell value. Add a .Formula after the Excel.Cell().

```
'NOW returns the current date and time
Excel.Cells(2,13).Formula= "=NOW()"

'Specify date format for NOW formula
Excel.Cells(2,13).NumberFormat = "m/d/yyyy"
```

Some Excel formulas require quotation marks. If this is the case you will have to use Chr(34) character representation instead.

```
Excel.Cells(1,9).Formula="=SUMIF(I5:I"&RwNum+2 &","&Chr(34)&">0"&Chr(34)&")"
```

Now, let's combine a For Loop with a couple of SUM and IF formulas.

```
Dim RwNumX As Integer
RwNumX=1

For x=1 to RwNum

        Excel.Cells(RwNumX,11).Formula =
        "=SUM($J$2:J"&RwNumX &")"

        Excel.Cells(RwNumX,12).Formula= "=IF(J"&RwNumX &"=0,
        M1,K"&RwNumX&")"
Next 'x
```

Defining Excel Constants

Excel contains several values as constants which we will need to define in our code in order for our macro to work correctly. These constants may pertain to the border of a cell, if the text is centered vertically or horizontally, etc. Listed below are a few common constant values. Use Excel's VBA editor to find the constant value you are looking for.

```
Const xlCenter = -4108          Const xlEdgeBottom = 9
Const xlAscending = 1           Const xlSolid = 1
Const xlYes = 1                 Const xlAutomatic = -4105
Const xlSortOnValues = 0        Const xlThemeColorDark1 = 1
Const xlSortNormal = 0          Const xlContinuous = 1
Const xlTopToBottom = 1         Const xlDiagonalUp = 6
Const xlPinYin = 1              Const xlDiagonalDown = 5
Const xlDown = -4121            Const xlThin = 2
Const xlBottom = -4107          Const xlNone = -4142
Const xlThick = 4               Const xlEdgeRight = 10
```

Inserting Rows and Columns

Inserting new rows and columns into your spreadsheet is very easy. First, select a cell in the spreadsheet and then specify if you want to insert a row above it as in these examples:

```
'insert a row at the top for headers
Excel.Cells(1,1).Select
Excel.ActiveCell.EntireRow.Insert

'Insert column to the left of the active cell
Excel.ActiveCell.EntireColumn.Insert

'Insert column to the right of the active cell
Excel.Cells(1,8).Select
Excel.ActiveCell.EntireColumn.Offset(0, 1).Insert
```

Sorting the Excel Spreadsheet

Parts listed under a product in CATIA may not be in numerical order. It is very easy to sort these part numbers in Excel.

```
'sort parts in numerical order G1, then sort by fasteners A1
Excel.Range("A:G").Select
Excel.Selection.Sort
Excel.Range("G1"),1,Excel.Range("A1"),,1,Excel.Range("B1"),1,1,1,False
```

Deleting Rows and Columns

Sometimes it is helpful to create extra columns in your spreadsheet to help with sorting, but they are not needed and can be removed at the end. To delete a row or column in your exported Excel file, activate the sheet and specify the row or column number to be deleted.

```
'delete 2nd row because it is empty
Excel.ActiveWorkbook.ActiveSheet.Rows(2).Delete
'delete sorter column G
Excel.ActiveWorkbook.ActiveSheet.Columns(7).Delete
```

Formatting Excel

After all the formulas and sorting on the spreadsheet is complete, then it's time to format to get it the way you want it to look. I recommend leaving the formatting until the end. Some formatting examples:

```
'Select range to format
      Excel.Rows("1:1").Select
'change font to bold
      Excel.Selection.Font.Bold = True
'change font size to 12
      Excel.Selection.Font.Size = 12

'change the font type, size, borders, colors, text wrap, etc.
With Excel.Range("A"&"1", "G"&RwNum)

.Font.Name = "Arial"
.Font.Size = 9
.HorizontalAlignment = xlCenter
.VerticalAlignment = xlCenter
.ColumnWidth = 25
.RowHeight = 20
.Borders.LineStyle = xlContinuous
.Borders.Weight = xlThick
.Borders.ColorIndex = 1
.WrapText = True
.EntireColumn.Autofit

End With


'merge cells in selected range
Excel.Range("Z1:AA1").Select
Excel.Selection.Merge

'wrap text within selected range
Excel.Range("W3","AA3").WrapText = True

'change the font color to red
Excel.Cells(2,12).Font.Color = -16776961
```

To insert a diagonal line through a cell use the following code:

```
Excel.Range("K"&Last,"M"&Last).Select
Excel.Selection.Borders(xlDiagonalDown).LineStyle = xlNone
With Excel.Selection.Borders(xlDiagonalUp)
.LineStyle = xlContinuous
.ColorIndex = 1
.TintAndShade = 0
.Weight = xlThin
End With
```

Change the entire sheet background color to white:

```
Excel.Cells.Select
With Excel.Selection.Interior
.Pattern = xlSolid
.PatternColorIndex = xlAutomatic
```

```
.ThemeColor = xlThemeColorDark1
.TintAndShade = 0
.PatternTintAndShade = 0
End With
```

Excel Charts

To insert a data chart in Excel use:
```
Charts.Add
```

Next, associate your cell values to the chart using:
```
ActiveChart.SetSourceData
```

Finally, position the chart within your Excel sheet with:
```
ActiveChart.Location
```

To learn more about Microsoft Excel functions and VBA, I recommend reading the **Excel 2010 Bible by John Walkenbach.**

Excel to CATIA

Alternatively, code can be written in Excel and data can be sent to CATIA. Open the VBA editor (link in the Developer tab or Alt+F11) and insert a new module. Again, make sure all the CATIA libraries are selected under Tools>References. The name of the Sub does not have to be CATMain or anything special. In the following example, we'll enter the code in Excel, launch CATIA, create a new product with two parts, and then populate the instance name and nomenclature fields from the data in our Excel file.

```
Sub ExcelToCatia()
'obtain the Catia object
    Dim CATIA As INFITF.Application
    On Error Resume Next
    Set CATIA = GetObject(, "CATIA.Application")
    If Err.Number <> 0 Then
        Set CATIA = CreateObject("CATIA.application")
        CATIA.Visible = True
    End If
    On Error GoTo 0
```

```
    'active worksheet
    Dim oWB As Excel.Workbook
    Set oWB = Excel.ActiveWorkbook
    Dim oSh As Excel.Worksheet
    Set oSh = oWB.ActiveSheet

    'create a new product
    Dim oProdDoc As ProductDocument
    Set oProdDoc = CATIA.Documents.Add("Product")

    Dim oRootProd As Product
    Set oRootProd = oProdDoc.Product

    'rename newly created product to "Example"
    oRootProd.PartNumber = "Example"

    Dim oProductsRoot As Products
    Set oProductsRoot = oRootProd.Products

    'create a new part named Test
    Dim newPart As Product
    Set newPart = oProductsRoot.AddNewComponent("Part", "Test")

    Dim newPart2 As Product
    Set newPart2 = oProductsRoot.AddNewComponent("Part", "Test2")

    'push data to from Excel to Catia. Instance name is in column b
    Dim i As Integer
    For i = 1 To oProductsRoot.Count
        Dim oProduct As Product
        Set oProduct = oProductsRoot.Item(i)
        oProduct.Name = oSh.Range("B" & 1 + i).Value
'nomenclature data is in column c starting in row 2
        oProduct.Nomenclature = oSh.Range("C" & 1 + i).Value
    Next

    'Update the product
    oRootProd.Update

End Sub
```

Export to Microsoft Power Point

Before launching PowerPoint we need to declare all of our objects and variables, including declaring the PowerPoint application. The following code creates a new PowerPoint application if none are opened or starts a new presentation if PowerPoint is already being used.

```
'export to PowerPoint
Dim oPPT As Object
Set oPPT=CreateObject("PowerPoint.Application")

        On Error Resume Next
        Set oPPT = GetObject("PowerPoint.Application")

        If Err.Number <> 0 Then
        Set oPPT = New PowerPoint.Application

End If
```

First, Dim or declare the PowerPoint presentation, and slides. We will also maximize the window and prepare to add new, blank slides to the presentation.

```
Dim oPPTPres As PowerPoint.Presentation
Dim oPPSlides As PowerPoint.Slides
Dim oPPSlide1, oPPSlide2, oPPSlide3 As PowerPoint.Slide
oPPT.WindowState=WindowMaximized
Set oPPTPres=oPPT.Presentations.Add()
```

Now, we are going to add a title slide to our PowerPoint presentation. There are a number of different slide styles you can add, which is designated by the second number inside the parenthesis after the "Add." The first number is the slide number. You can also set the header text box of the slide to display the part name of your CATIA object or any other custom text.

```
'title slide
Set objSlide = oPPTPres.Slides.Add(1, 1)
objSlide.Shapes(1).TextFrame.TextRange.Text = partName
objSlide.Shapes(2).TextFrame.TextRange.Text = "Annotation Data"
```

It is often useful to add images captured from the 3D model into your PPT. We do this by inserting our image capture macro code within out PowerPoint exporter.

```
Dim viewer1 As Viewer
Set viewer1= CATIA.ActiveWindow.ActiveViewer
```

VB Scripting for CATIA V5

```
Dim viewpoint1 As Viewpoint3D
Set viewpoint1= viewer1.Viewpoint3D

Dim ObjViewer3D As Viewer3D
Set objViewer3D = CATIA.ActiveWindow.ActiveViewer
```

If you want to add ten slides to your ppt, set i=10 and use a For Loop. Use the i value again to add new slides to the end of the slideshow.

```
Dim objSlide As PowerPoint.Slide
Set objSlide = oPPTPres.Slides.Add(i+1, 36)
'capnamer is the name of the catpart

objSlide.Shapes(1).TextFrame.TextRange.Text = capNamer

Set pic=objSlide.Shapes.AddPicture(strName, False, True,_
50, 5, 576, 350)
```

Adding headers and footer automatically to your presentation is very easy. Common footers to add include slide number, date, time, presenter name, company name, etc.

```
objSlide.HeadersFooters.Footer.Visible = True
objSlide.HeadersFooters.Footer.Text = partName
objSlide.HeadersFooters.DateAndTime.Visible = True

objSlide.HeadersFooters.DateAndTime.UseFormat = True
objSlide.HeadersFooters.DateAndTime.Format = 1
objSlide.HeadersFooters.SlideNumber.Visible = True
```

If you insert image captures into your slideshow they may not be the right size so you might have to adjust them manually. Before you make modifications, it is a good idea to lock the aspect ratio. Use this code to lock the aspect ratio for all the pictures as you insert them:

```
Pic.LockAspectRatio=True
```

At the end of your code you will probably want to make PowerPoint visible:

```
oPPT.Visible =True
```

Now you can export data from CATIA V5 to Microsoft's PowerPoint!

Microsoft Office Word

In addition to Excel and PowerPoint, Microsoft Word can also be launched from inside of CATIA using a VBScript. To create and open a new word document with the text "Welcome to your new document":

```
Dim eptWord As Word.Application
On Error Resume Next
    Set eptWord=GetObject(,"Word.Application")
        If Err<>0Then
        Set eptWord=CreateObject("Word.Application")
        eptWord.Visible=True
    End If
Set myDoc=eptWord.Documents.Add(DocumentType:=wdNewBlankDocument)
d.Range.Text="Welcome to your new document!"
```

Chapter 11: Examples

One of the best ways to learn is by example. For learning as well as efficiency, many programmers like to take code from a macro they know already works and then modify it to fit their specific needs. Feel free to use these codes and do the same.

Display the Density of a Part

The "&" symbol works much the same as the concatenate formula in Microsoft Excel by combining multiple elements. For example, if you want a pop up message box to read "The density is 55" where 55 is a variable which will update with the part try this code:

```
Sub CATMain()

    Dim productDocument1 As Document
    Set productDocument1 = CATIA.ActiveDocument

    Dim partRoot As Document
    Set partRoot = productDocument1.Part

        MsgBox "The density is " & partRoot.Density

End Sub
```

'Display the volume of an assembly

```
Msgbox oProdDoc.Product.Analyze.Volume
```

To print a document on your default printer:
```
CATIA.ActiveWindow.PrintOut
```

To get the coordinates of the center of gravity:
```
Analyze.GetGravityCenter()
```

To get the mass of a product:
```
Analyze.Mass
```

Display number of solid bodies in a part:

```
    Dim oPartDoc As PartDocument
    Set oPartDoc = Part1.CATPart
    Msgbox oPartDoc.Part.Bodies.Count
```

136

OR

```
Dim Bod As Bodies
Set Bod = oPartDoc.Part.Bodies
Msgbox Bod.Count
```
Incorrect (don't make this common mistake): msgbox Bod.Collection.Count

Windows Explorer

To open an Explorer window relative to the CATIA Active Document path:

```
Sub CATMain()
Set wshShell = CreateObject("WScript.Shell")
wshShell.Run "explorer.exe " & CATIA.ActiveDocument.Path
End Sub
```


Execute a Macro on CATIA Startup

To begin running a macro immediately upon CATIA startup, add the word "-marco" to the CATIA start command. Use this syntax to run macro "STARTER":

```
CNEXT -macro STARTER.catvbs
CNEXT -macro STARTER.CATScript
CNEXT -macro STARTER.catvba
CNEXT -macro STARTER.CATPart
```

Execute a macro from within other macros by using this line of code:
```
CATIA.SystemService.ExecuteScript
```


Design Mode

If you're working with large assemblies, you may want to automatically set each item in the tree to design mode (individually opened parts are typically automatically opened in design mode already):

```
Dim productDocument1 As Document
Dim product1 As Product
Dim products1 As Products

Set productDocument1=CATIA.ActiveDocument
```

```
Set product1 = productDocument1.Product
Set products1 = product1.Products
Products1.item(i).ApplyWorkMode DESIGN_MODE
```

Often times when you are dealing with a very large assembly in CATIA the files are setup so that when you open these huge assemblies the parts and products come in as CGR files in visualization mode. To begin working on a part you need to switch the part and products into design mode. This can be accomplished with an easy CATScript macro. In this example, we will check to see if the top level product document is in design mode. If not then we will display a message box asking the user's permission to automatically switch the product document to design mode.

```
Sub CATMain()
Dim prdRoot As Product
Set prdroot = CATIA.ActiveDocument.Product
'check if a product is in Design Mode
If (prdRoot.PartNumber = "") Then' propose user to switch it in design mode
Dim vbResponse
vbResponse = MsgBox("Product " & prdRoot.Name & " is not in design mode. Would
you like to switch it?", vbYesNo, "Warning")If (vbResponse = vbYes) Then
prdRoot.ApplyWorkMode DESIGN_MODE
End If
Else
Msgbox "product already in design mode"
End If
End Sub
```

As usual in CATIA, there are multiple ways to accomplish the same task. Another method could be this:

```
Product_activ = InputBox("Is the active Assembly in Design Mode ? Yes (Y) or
No_ (N)_!", "Product representations", "Yes")
If Product_activ = "" Then
MsgBox " Yes (Y) or No (N) ?"
'insert goto desired resulting action here
Else
If Product_activ = "N" Or Product_activ = "n" Then
' goto end sub
Else
End If
End If
```

This code by itself may not be very important to you but it might be a very good idea to add this to the beginning of a more complex macro designed to modify geometry or something else where the product must be in design mode first. As a programmer, you can never assume anything. Don't assume the parts will already be in design mode. Make sure your code first checks for design mode and then switch to it if needed. This will save you a lot of time later on when other, less experienced users begin running your code and can't get it to work because of something simple like being in design mode or not.

138

Activation State

The following returns the activation state (active or de-active) of a product:

```
Function GetActivationState(ByVal aProduct As Product)
As Boolean
Dim oParameter As BoolParam
    Set oParameter =
aProduct .Parameters.Item(mProduct.Parent.Parent.PartNum
ber & "\" & aProduct .Name & "\" & "Component Activation
State")
    Return oParameter.Value()
End Function
```

Identify a Part or Product

A useful code you may find helpful is to identify whether a file is a CATProduct or a CATPart. One method is like this:

```
Dim parentFileName As String

parentFileName=products1.item(i).ReferenceProduct.Parent.name

'If the file name contains ".CATProduct" then loop
'through the child parts

    If Instr(parenFileName, ".CATProduct")<>0 Then

Else
```

In order to go from a known "Product" object to get the "PartDocument" and "Part" that are associated with it you need to go through the GetMasterShapeRepresentation method

```
Dim prod1 As Product
'Assume that prod1 gets set to an instance here
Dim partDoc1 As PartDocument
Set partDoc1 = prod1.GetMasterShapeRepresentation(True)
Dim part1 as Part
Set part1 = partDoc1.Part
```

To create a new part in the Assembly, you would use the AddNewComponent method

```
Dim objProduct As Product
Set objProduct = objRootProduct.Products.AddNewComponent("Part","NewPart")
```

Keep in mind, that when the new part is added, the objProduct object will reference the "Product" level of the Part. The Product class in CATIA VBA has a peculiar property called

"ReferenceProduct". This property returns a Product.

Also, there are two internal names for products inside CATIA V5: the Product Name and the Instance Name. These can both be accessed via the CATIA Object Model using two different properties:

Example: SubAssy1(SubAssy1.1) where the product name is SubAssy1 and the instance name is AubAssy1.1:
Product Name: `objProduct.Name`
Instance Name: `objProduct.PartNumber`

Products and Components

Products in CATIA are shown with a white piece of paper. These assemblies have a CATProduct file that is saved on the hard drive and can be sent somewhere else.

Components in CATIA show no piece of paper and do NOT have a CATProduct file.

To add a product with a physical file:

```
Dim oProduct As Product
Set oProduct = oRootProduct.Products.AddNewComponent("Product", "Assembly1")
```

To add a new component without a physical file:

```
Dim oProduct As Product
Set oProduct =
oRootProduct.Products.AddNewProduct("A
ssembly1")
```

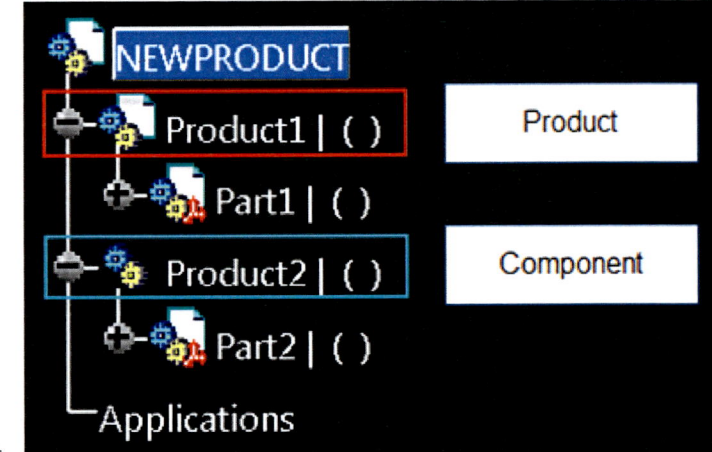

Description

How do you return a CATPart or CATProduct description with a macro? Using VB scripting you can use the following CATScript code to loop through all the parts within a product assembly and return what the description is. When you right click on a part within an assembly you will actually see two description boxes - component and product.

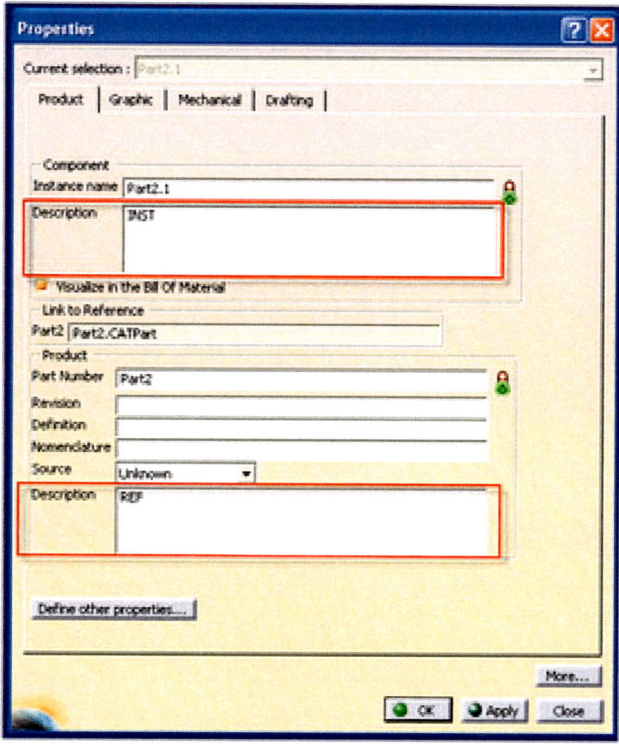

The top description name in the box is for the component level and can be called using **DescriptionInst** which returns or sets the product's description for a component product. The bottom description name is for the product and is found through our script using **DescriptionRef** which set's the product's description for a reference product and is a property in the object product. Getting the part description may be useful in creating bills of materials or other part list documents.

```
Sub CATMain()
Dim productDocument1 As Document
Dim product1 As Product
Dim products1 As Products
Set productDocument1 = CATIA.ActiveDocument

Set product1 = productDocument1.Product
Set products1 = product1.Products

'count the number of CATParts within the catproduct

partcount=product1.Products.Count
msgbox"CHECK: The number of parts is "&partcount&". Please click OK to_
continue."

Dim i As Integer
```

```
'loop through all parts
For i=1 to partcount

'apply design mode to each part
products1.Item(i).ApplyWorkMode DESIGN_MODE

Dim partDoc1 As PartDocument
Set partDoc1=products1.Item(i)

Dim getDes, getDes2 As String
getDes = partDoc1.DescriptionInst
getDes2 = partDoc1.DescriptionRef

Msgbox "Component description is " & getDes& " and Product Description " & _
getDes2

Next 'i
End Sub
```

To rename (or to enter a new name) to your part description field use this code by adding it to the above text during the i loop, before Next and after the msgbox:

```
partDoc1.DescriptionRef = "Test"

partDoc1.DescriptionInst = "CompTest"&i
```

The first line will add "Test" to each product description field while the second line will add "CompTest" and the loop number. So for the first part in your assembly where i=1, after running the macro the component description will read "CompTest1", the next part "CompTest2" and so on.

Parent Name

The following macro is referred to as "What is this?" as it returns the name and type of a selected element. This is a good macro to use when you are not sure if a part is referred to as "Part" or "CATPart" or if a point is "Point" or "HybridShapePoint". It tells me what the selected geometry is!

```
Option Explicit
Sub CATMain()
Dim oSel As Selection
```

142

```
Set oSel = CATIA.ActiveDocument.Selection
 MsgBox "Selected: " & oSel.Count
    Dim i As Integer

    For i = 1 To oSel.Count

        Dim oSelEl As SelectedElement
        Set oSelEl = oSel.Item(i)

        MsgBox "Name " & oSelEl.Value.Name
        MsgBox "Type " & oSelEl.Type


        MsgBox "Parent Name " & oSelEl.Value.Parent.Name
        MsgBox "Parent Type " & TypeName(oSelEl.Value.Parent)
        Next i

 oSel.Clear

End Sub
```

Chapter 12: Troubleshooting and Tips

Creating your first Custom Macro

You're probably ready to begin creating your first custom CATIA macro. This means you've completed all the step-by-step tutorials and now want to create something from scratch on your own. While it's easy to follow along with examples, it's much more difficult when starting from nothing. When many beginners go to write their first macro they don't know where to start. Listed below is the process I use when beginning any new macro, whether I'm making it for myself or someone else. The first thing you need to do is to come up with a plan by asking yourself these important questions:

1. What would be the ideal macro solution be? This is always the first question I ask myself or my client when dealing with a complicated issue. Now, the ideal solution may in fact be impossible to obtain but at least we now have a clear, established goal to aspire towards.

2. What CATIA programming language you are most comfortable coding in: .catvbs, .CATScript, or .catvba? There are advantages and disadvantages to each macro language and it really comes down to what is the design intent.

3. What step by step process should the macro follow? Next, I want to get an overall idea of how the macro should work. It also helps to think about the steps the macro will need to perform. I often write out a flowchart, decision tree, or quickly sketch a process map.

Just like any other general engineering challenge, I like to take seemingly large problems and try to break them down into smaller, easier to solve components then put them all together again in the end for the final solution. I break the big problem down into smaller problems by asking more detailed questions, like:

4. Will this macro be used only on individual parts, or products? What will the active document be?

Example: If you're dealing with a single part you will more than likely begin with:

```
Dim partDocument As Document
Set partDocument = CATIA.ActiveDocument
Dim oPart As Part
Set oPart = partDocument.Part
```

Or, if you're dealing with a product:

```
Dim prodDocument As Document
Set prodDocument = CATIA.ActiveDocument
Dim oProd As Product
Set oProd = prodDocument.Product
```

There are instances, such as when you are taking a screen capture, where it doesn't matter what the active document is.

5. What steps or inputs will the user need to do? What information will the macro need to run? Most macros should be as easy as possible for the end user with minimal inputs – otherwise what is the point of automating the process if it takes a long time to set up?

Example: if a macro is going to translate a bunch of points, will the points be selected by a user before the macro is run, will the user manually select the points while the program is running, or will the macro use a search function to select them by name with no direct user interaction? These are the type of things you need to think about before diving into the programming.

Troubleshooting - What To Do If You Get Stuck

You're trying to write your first CATIA macro and you've answered all the questions you needed to ask before you began but now you're simply stuck and don't know what to do next. Or maybe you've already written some code but it's just not working the way you intended it to. How in the world are we supposed to go on from this point? If you're new to CATIA programming you're likely going to be dead in the water at this point until you get some help.

Before giving up, there are a few steps I recommend you take to try and figure the solution out for yourself. I strongly believe you learn more through struggling, overcoming obstacles, and doing it yourself. Here is my list of things you should do if you consider yourself stuck writing a CATIA macro:

1. Use the Macro Recorder

The first step I recommend you to try if you're stuck writing a CATIA macro is to use the macro recorder to record your actions of doing the process manually just to get an idea of what the code might look like. Start the macro recorder, perform the action, then look at the recorded code to get an idea of what the code looks like, then modify the program so it will work on other parts all the time. Remember, recorded macros do not contain any comments or explanations of what is happening in the code and input parameters are never recorded. There are no loops either.

I generally only use the macro recorder as a guide because it usually records a lot of extra lines of code that aren't needed. This is based on the order of steps that you do as you record the macro. These unnecessary lines can be removed One way for you to learn what is needed is to comment out a line of code (by inserting an apostrophe at the beginning of the line) and then running the macro to see if it still works properly.

2. CATIA Object Browser

CATIA has two built in features that can potentially help you solve your problems. The first is the CATIA object browser and is a great tool to use when you're stuck and don't know what to do next. While in the CATScript editor go to View>Object Browser (or simply hit F2) and use the search bar. Documentation can be found from within the CATIA VBA editor by way of the menu. Go to View>Object Browser or simply hit F2.

Let's say you want to figure out how to create a new rib feature. Open the VBA Object Browser and type "rib" into the search bar. Look in the third column ("member") for anything something that makes sense, in this case "AddNewRib" looks good. The second column ("class") will tell you what object is needed to use the function. At the bottom of the window you'll see how to use the function and what inputs are needed.

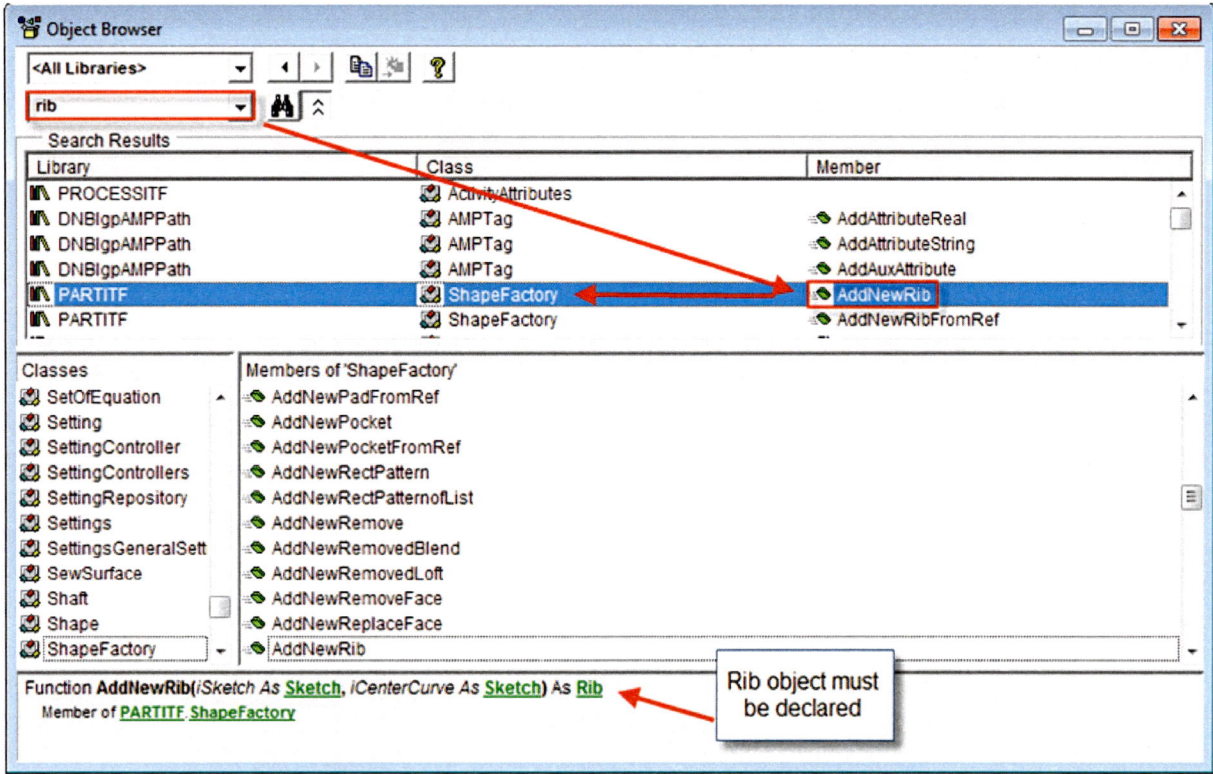

3. CATIA Visual Basic Help Documentation

The other built-in feature is the CATIA Visual Basic Help Documentation (also known as CATIA Automation Documentation) that can be accessed using either the online help (if the complete CATIA Documentation is not installed) or by opening the file:

<Catia_install_folder>\intel_a\code\biV5Automation.chm.

Navigate to the directory B18\intel_a\code\bin, right-click on the file V5Automation.chm, and choose "Create Shortcut", which will create a shortcut to this file in this same directory. Move the shortcut to your desktop and double-click on it to open it.

To navigate the CATIA object diagram click on the "Contents" tab, expand the CAA V5 Visual Basic Reference node and then select CAA V5 Objects. The CATIA Object Diagram shown in the help files is colored coded and distinguishes objects from abstract objects and collections.

- The cyan color denotes a single object.
- The purples color denotes an abstract object.
- The yellow color denotes a collection.
- Click the red arrow to expand the diagram to the next level.

Connections with arrows denote inheritance while connector without arrows shows aggregation. Although it is not shown in the CATIA object model diagram, the PartDocument object aggregates both the Part and Product objects.

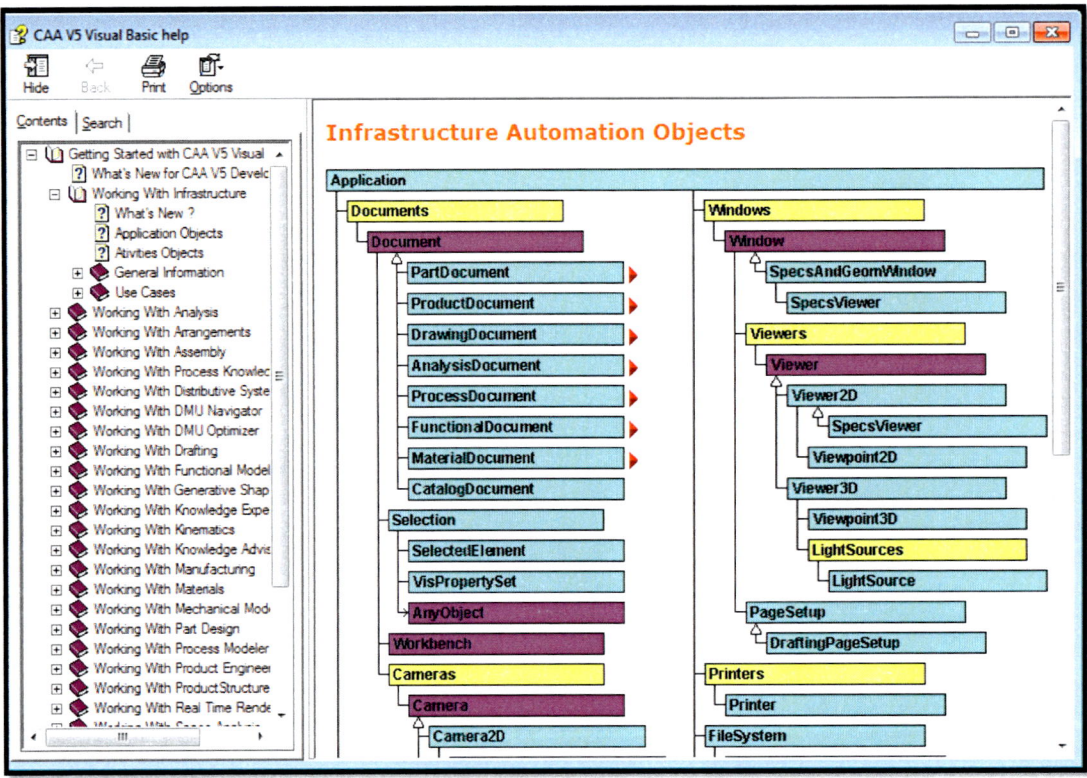

After opening the .chm file, click on the "PartDocument" element of the diagram, which should navigate to the API documentation of the PartDocument class. The API documentation shows the inheritance tree, and a listing of the Properties and Methods of the PartDocument class. Note there is no "Close" method listed. This is because the "Close" method is inherited from the Document class. To see all of the methods available for a particular class, you should check every class that it inherits from up to "AnyObject". Classes above that are not of any interest. To navigate back to the CATIA object diagram, click on the "Contents" tab, expand the "CAA V5 Visual Basic Reference" node, and select "CAA V5 Objects."

Online help documentation is another source of API documentation. The Automation Documentation is found under the "Infrastructure" Icon. There is also a special set of On-Line help that is available with the CAA RADE interfaces (it's on this CD). A RADE license is NOT required to access the help files. Read through all the workshops for a better understanding of how to navigate the documentation.

4. Look at other code as examples

A great way to learn is to see how other programmers solved similar problems. Be sure to read through all examples in this book as well as on my website(http://www.scripting4v5.com) as many of them have thorough explanations of how they work. Online forums, such as the ones listed in the Tools and Resources appendix, are also a great place to see CATIA macro examples.

5. Step away from the problem

This is actually my favorite tip here. There has been countless times where I've been banging my head against a wall, not able to figure out a problem. So, I would simply get up from my computer and walk away, maybe for a few hours or days, and not think about the problem at all. Then when I sit down in front of the screen again refreshed the answer hits me almost immediately. Seriously, this happens almost every time! It's that whole not being able to see the forest through the trees type of thing. So take a break!

6. Use the Internet to Ask Questions

Google is your friend! If you don't find a suitable answer on your first search try a new one with different words. Personally, there's nothing that annoys me more than when someone asks me a question and I simply Google it and I find the solution right away. Don't be lazy! Other people do not want to do your work for you.

If you're still stuck and clueless about what to do next you can ask for help from another programmer or automation expert. Posting in the recommend forums listed on my Resources page is a great way to get feedback from multiple power users.

Debugging Tips

One way to debug a VBA program is to create a break point. To create a breakpoint for debugging a program, click in the grey bar near the line of code at the point where you wish to break the execution of the program. The program will stop temporarily at the break point enabling you to view the variables at that point. The program can be executed line by line to check the flow and other values. To quit a running VBA application use the End command.

All User Forms in VBA have a Show method. When you call this method a Form is displayed on the screen enabling the user to use the Controls in the Form to work with the VBA application. Use this code:

```
UserForm1.Show
```

Compile error: Function or interface marked as restricted or the function uses an Automation type not supported in Visual Basic.

To work around this error you need to create a "dummy" variable and assign the specific object to the new dummy object which does not have a specific type. Use the dummy object to call the method.

Dim dummy

Set dummy = sketch1

Dummy.SetLineType

Different CATIA Versions

If there are multiple versions of CATIA V5 on your computer, you can find out which one is registered by looking at the directory. To automate a specific version of CATIA you first have to register that version with Windows. Here are the steps to un-register or re- register a CATIA V5 version (Please note this only needs to be done between full releases and not service packs!)

1. Reboot your pc
2. Open a command prompt
3. CD to the unload directory of the version of CATIA you want to un-register
   (i.e. "c\program files\Dassault systemes\B15\intel_a\code\bin")
4. Run the command "cnext-unregserver"
5. Open up the task manager and wait until the "cnext" process stops running (which may take a few minutes)
6. CD to the unload directory of the version of CATIA you want to register
   (i.e. "c\program files\Dassault systems\B16\intel_a\code\bin")
7. Run the command "cnext-regserver"
8. In the task manager again, wait until the "cnext" process stops

9. Open up VB and check that the correct version is registered

To find out the version, release, and service packs of the CATIA session you are working in run this code:

```
MsgBox "V" & CATIA.SystemConfiguration.Version & _
       "R" & CATIA.SystemConfiguration.Release & _
       "(SP" & CATIA.SystemConfiguration.ServicePack & ")"
```

Registering CATIA Libraries

When CATIA is installed, CATIA libraries are automatically registered in the Windows registry. In addition to the standard VBA and CATIA APIs there are a number of additional APIs that you can access in your VBA programs.

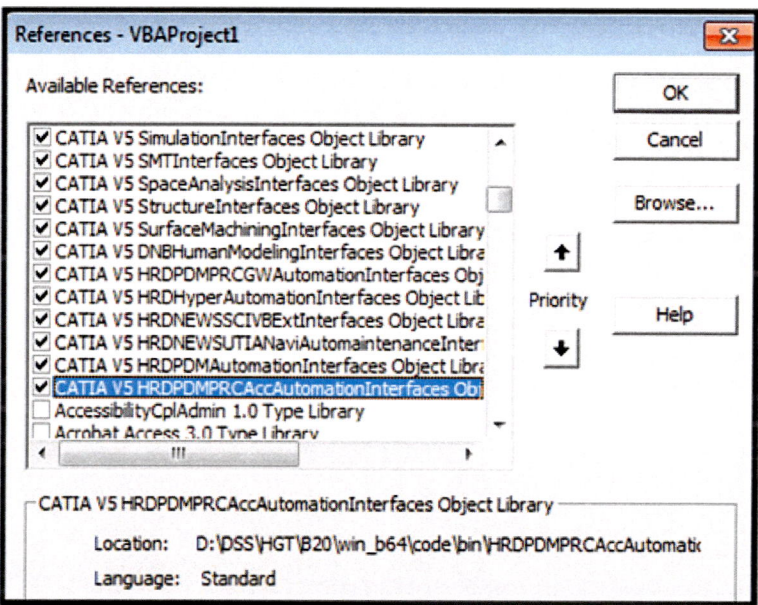

By default there are a large number of CATIA references which are selected. Each reference is actually a type library (.tlb) located in the CATIA "bin" directory. Some of the most important additional references commonly used are the Microsoft Office application object libraries.

Tips to Make Your Macros Run Faster

To make your CATScript macro run faster turn off the refresh display while the macro is running then turn it back on once it is complete, like so:

```
Sub CATMain()
CATIA.RefreshDisplay = False
'enter code here
CATIA.RefreshDisplay = True
End Sub
```

You may also want to hide any file alerts (such as a dialog box that pops up notifying the user that the file they need to save is read only). Turn them on and off like this:

```
CATIA.DisplayFileAlerts = False
CATIA.DisplayFileAlerts = True
```

You can also change the size of the window to force CATIA to refresh or repaint. In this example, we will change the width of the window by two (may not be detectable to the eye) and reset it back to the original width (which is expressed in pixels):

```
Sub CATMain()
CATIA.RefreshDisplay = True
iWidth = CATIA.ActiveWindow.Width
CATIA.ActiveWindow.Width = iWidth - 2
CATIA.ActiveWindow.Width = iWidth
End Sub
```

Tips and Reminders

A few tips and tricks as well as other important reminders:

- When using forms be sure to name your command buttons, text boxes, etc. before you begin coding because it will not automatically update the code if you change an item's name.
- You can hide CATIA visibility while running a program to increase the speed of the program.
- Leave comments so your source code should read like a book. That way, if you or someone else looks at the code a year down the right you will be able to quickly know why you did what you did.

- To register type libraries in VBA go to Tools>References and select all the libraries you want to use in the project. For CATIA VB programs all of the CATIA type libraries should be selected. Type libraries are .TLB files.
- All arrays start from 0. All collections start from 1 (i.e. Loops).
- For CATIA V5 running on UNIX, emulators allow for VBScripts to be run with no interface building tools. Some CATScripts from this text may work under UNIX OS but not all due to differences between the two systems.
- To see what unit abbreviations CATIA uses go to Tools>Options>Parameters and Measures>Units.
- To search through all use ,all but to search through only a selection use ,sel.
- Global variables are defined as Public.
- On Error Resume Next does not fix errors, it merely ignores them.
- To quit a running VBA application use the End command.
- If your code doesn't work in VBA, try copy and pasting it into CATScript or MS VBScript.
- You can change the default macro editor by going to Tools>Options>Macros>Default Editor. For example, you could change it from the default to Notepad.exe (shown below).

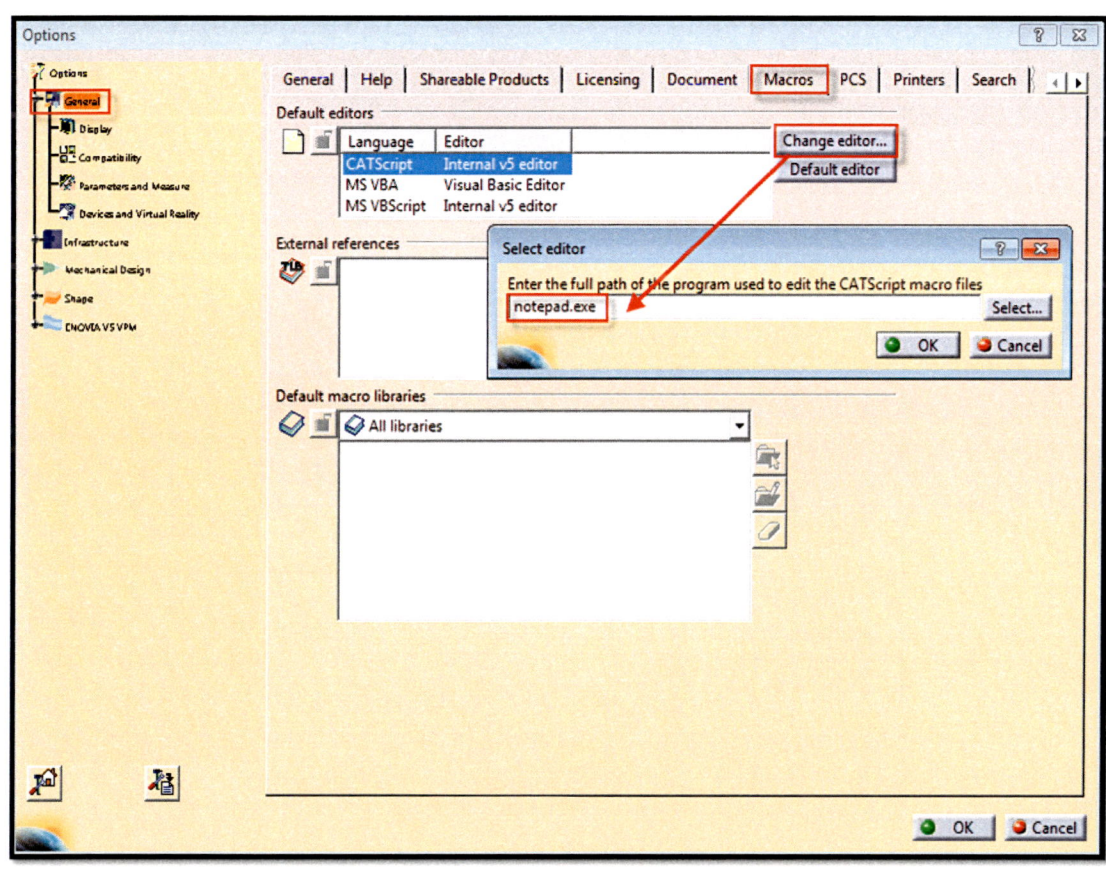

Chapter 13: Final Thoughts

Now you know how to program macros for CATIA V5! You're on your way to automating those repetitive processes and impressing your coworkers and bosses. For more real world examples, articles, tutorials, and how-to videos please visit www.scripting4v5.com

I hope you've enjoyed this eBook as much as I loved writing it for you. I can't thank you enough for your continued support of scripting4v5.com and everything I do. I appreciate each and every one of you for taking time out of your day or evening to read this, and if you have an extra second, **I would love to hear what you think about it.** Please leave a comment at *http://www.scripting4v5.com*, or if you'd rather reach me in private, don't hesitate to shoot me an email. I read each and every single comment and email, so don't be afraid to say hi!

I've worked very hard on this guide and spent countless hours working on the website and simply ask that you do not share this document with anyone who has not purchased it. Please refer all friends and colleagues to my website, www.scripting4v5.com.

To all of my subscribers, followers and friends out there, old and new, thank you for the gift of your support. I only hope this guide can begin to repay you for the time and attention that you've given me. Here's to you and your continued success!

Thanks again, good luck, and happy programming!

-Emmett Ross

Chapter 14: Exercise Solutions

Listed below are the solutions to each of the exercise presented in the book. Remember, there are multiple ways to code so if yours doesn't exactly match that doesn't necessarily mean it's wrong, as long as the end result accomplishes the goal.

Exercise 5.1 Delete a Geometrical Set

```
'CATScript
Sub CATMain()

Dim partDocument1 As Document
Set partDocument1 = CATIA.ActiveDocument

Dim selection1 As Selection
Set selection1 = partDocument1.Selection

'clear the selection
selection1.Clear

Dim part1 As Part
Set part1 = partDocument1.Part

Dim hybridBodies1 As HybridBodies
Set hybridBodies1 = part1.HybridBodies

Dim hybridBody1 As HybridBody
Set hybridBody1 = hybridBodies1.Item("GEOMETRIC SET 1")

'set GEOMETRIC SET 1 as the selection
selection1.Add hybridBody1

'delete the geometric set
selection1.Delete

End Sub
```

Exercise 5.2 Paste Special:

```
'CATScript

Sub CATMain()

    Dim oDoc As CATIA.ActiveDocument
    Set oDoc = CATIA.ActiveDocument

    Dim oSel As Selection
    Set oSel = oDoc.Selection

    Dim GSet1 As HybridBody
    Set GSet1 = oDoc.Part.HybridBodies.Item(1)
    oSel.Add GSet1
    oSel.Copy

    'create the new part
    Dim part2
    Set part2 = CATIA.Documents.Add("CATPart")

    'rename the new part
    Part2.Product.PartNumber = "Weld Station"

    'set the destination
    Dim GSet2 As HybridBody
    Set GSet2 = part2.Part.HybridBodies.Item(1)

    Dim partDoc2 As PartDocument
    Set partDoc2 = CATIA.ActiveDocument

    Dim ActSel As Selection
    Set ActSel = partDoc2.Selection
    ActSel.Add GSet2
    ActSel.PasteSpecial("CATPrtResultWithOutLink")
    'clear the selection
    ActSel.Clear

End Sub
```

Exercise 6.1 Delete Deactivated Features

```
'this CATScript macro deletes all deactive components (except for sketches)
'------------------------------------------------------------------------
Sub CATMain()

'error handling
On Error Resume Next

Dim partDocument1 'As Document
Set partDocument1 = CATIA.ActiveDocument

Dim part1 As Part
Set part1 = partDocument1.Part

If Err.Number=0 Then

        Dim selection1 'As Selection
        Set selection1 = partDocument1.Selection
      selection1.Search "CATPrtSearch.PartDesign Feature.Activity=FALSE"

        'if no deactivated components then end program
        If selection1.Count = 0 Then
                        Msgbox "No deactivated features."
                        Exit Sub
        Else

If MsgBox ("The number of deactivated components is: "&_
selection1.Count & ".  Click yes to delete or click no to exit.",_ vbYesNo) =
vbYes Then

'delete all deactivated components then update the part
                        selection1.Delete
                        part1.Update
                End If
        End If

'error handling
Else
        Msgbox "Not a part document! Open a single part document."
End If
End Sub
```

Exercise 7.1 Draw a 2D Circle:

```
'CATScript
Sub CATMain()

'catdrawing must be the activate document
Dim DrwDocument As DrawingDocument
Set DrwDocument = CATIA.ActiveDocument

Dim DrwSheets As DrawingSheets
Set DrwSheets = DrwDocument.Sheets


Dim DrwSheet As DrawingSheet
Set DrwSheet = DrwSheets.Item(1)


DrwSheet.Activate

Dim DrwView As DrawingView
Set DrwView = DrwSheet.Views.Item("Background View")


DrwView.Activate

Dim Fact As Factory2D
Set Fact = DrwView.Factory2D

'create the circle
Set Circle = Fact.CreateClosedCircle(50,100,100)

End Sub
```

Appendix I: Acronyms

The following terms are used throughout this text (in alphabetical order):

- **API**: Application Programming Interface
- **CAA**: CATIA Application Architecture
- **CAD**: Computer Aided Design
- **CATIA:** Computer Aided Three Dimensional Interactive Application
- **CLI:** Command Line Interface
- **COM**: Component Object Model
- **DLL**: Dynamic Linked Library
- **DMU:** Digital Mock-Up
- **GUI**: Graphical User Interface
- **IDE:** Integrated Development Environment
- **IDL:** Interface Definition Language
- **MDB**: Model Based Definition
- **OLE:** Object Linking and Embedding
- **OOP:** Object Oriented Programming
- **PBD**: Product Based Definition
- **PDM**: Product Data Management
- **PLM**: Product Lifecycle Management
- **RADE**: Rapid Application Development Environment
- **TLB**: Type Library File
- **UUID:** Universal Unique Identifier
- **VB6:** Visual Basic 6
- **VBA:** Visual Basic for Applications
- **VBE:** Visual Basic Editor

Appendix II: Keyboard Shortcuts

Default CATIA and VBA editor shortcuts:

CATIA V5:
- F1: Open the CATIA V5 online contextual help file
- Alt+F8: Macro shortcut
- Alt+F11: Open the macro editor

VBA Editor:
- F1: Visual Basic help
- F2: Open the Object Browser
- F4: Properties Window
- F5: Run macro
- F7: Code window
- F8: Step Into
- Crtl + Break: Break
- Crtl + J: List properties and methods
- Alt+F11: Go back to CATIA
- End: Quit a running macro

Appendix III: Tools and Resources

Below is a list of tools and resources I personally use (or have used) to help me with CATIA, programming, putting together this eBook, and creating my website. I highly recommend each and every one (and wouldn't list it here if I didn't). Some of these premium services do come with a price (just being honest here), but seriously I wouldn't risk mentioning them here if I didn't know they work great and will save a lot of people time and money.

Where to Get Your CATIA Macro Questions Answered

COE (CATIA Operators Exchange): Post your questions in the Develop and Deploy forum to get answers from knowledgeable and professional CATIA users. http://www.coe.org/p/fo/si/topic=113

Eng Tips Forum: Post your CATScript questions in the CATIA Products forum and get great feedback from CATIA power users.
http://www.eng-tips.com/threadminder.cfm?pid=560

StackOverFlow: Use this site to ask questions when you get stuck and there are tons of knowledgeable programmers willing to help you out.
http://stackoverflow.com/

Contact Me: I'll do my best to respond to you in a timely matter but due to the number of emails I get daily I may or may not be able to. Please be patient.
http://www.scripting4v5.com/Contact-Us/

CAD Resources

CAD Systems Help: If you have questions about CATIA other than macros or want to learn more about other CAD systems them subscribe to this blog.
http://cadsystemshelp.blogspot.com/

CATIA V5: The official Dassault Systèmes website.
http://www.3ds.com/

CATIA Jobs

oDesk: oDesk is a great website. You can find CAD jobs if you're looking for work or you can outsource work for freelancers, CAD designers, programmers, and others. Hire a virtual assistant and make life easier by lessoning your own workload.
http://www.odesk.com

Job Board: Visit our job board at scripting4v5.com to find CATIA design or CAD engineering related positions near you.
http://www.scripting4v5.com/catia-jobs/

CATIA, Programming, and Other Books

For more information on CATIA, VB Programming, or Microsoft Excel, I recommend checking out these resources from Amazon.com:

CATIA V5 R20 for Designers: An extremely detailed and helpful book, not just for beginners but intermediate and advanced 3D modelers and engineers as well.

Excel 2010 Bible by John Walkenbach: This is by far the best Excel book I have ever found for anyone who uses Microsoft Excel spreadsheets on a daily basis.

Introduction to CATIA V5 R19 (A hands-on Tutorial Approach): The tutorials seem to touch on every single icon that is available in CATIA and includes step-by-step tutorials with nice graphics.

Microsoft Visual Basic 2010 Step by Step by Michael Halvorson: A lot of hands-on work-by-examples will further the development of your Visual Basic programming skills.

Miscellaneous

Error Trapping with Visual Basic for Applications: Complete list of error codes when using the Err function.
http://support.microsoft.com/kb/146864

VBScript Functions: This page contains all the built in VBScript functions.

http://www.w3schools.com/vbscript/vbscript_ref_functions.asp

Excel Spreadsheets Help: Need help with Excel spreadsheets? Excel Spreadsheets Help has some of the best FREE Excel templates, especially for project management applications. Learn some useful macros by joining their email newsletter.

http://excelspreadsheetshelp.blogspot.com/

JustCloud: Backup and protect your computer files online in the cloud and access them from anywhere, at any time, from any device. I work on multiple computers and JustCloud makes it easy to work on the same files from many different locations.

http://www.scripting4v5.com/recommends/justcloud

Microsoft Excel Object Model: Microsoft's MSDN online library is the best place for finding out information about the Microsoft Office object model for VBA.

http://msdn.microsoft.com/en-us/library/wss56bz7(v=vs.80).aspx

Index

Made in the USA
Lexington, KY
22 December 2014